W9-CKL-771

TREVON JENIFER

FROM THE GROUND UP

Trevon Jenifer
with Alan Goldenbach

SP

SPORTS PUBLISHING L.L.C.

SportsPublishingLLC.com

ISBN-10: 1-59670-143-9
ISBN-13: 978-1-59670-143-4

Publishers: Peter L. Bannon and Joseph J. Bannon Sr.
Senior managing editor: Susan M. Moyer
Acquisitions editor: Mike Pearson
Developmental editor: Doug Hoepker
Art director: K. Jeffrey Higgerson
Dust jacket design: Dustin J. Hubbart
Interior layout: Dustin J. Hubbart
Photo editor: Erin Linden-Levy

Sports Publishing L.L.C.
804 North Neil Street
Champaign, IL 61820
Phone: 1-877-424-2665
Fax: 217-363-2073
SportsPublishingLLC.com

Printed in the United States of America

CIP data available upon request.

To the loving memory of Grandma Francine

—T.J.

To Elyse, my wonderful wife

—A.G.

ACKNOWLEDGMENTS

By Trevon Jenifer

I have thanked so many people throughout this book for helping me achieve all that I have. I would be careless, though, if I did not acknowledge the people whose time, generosity, and thoughtfulness were critical to making this book possible.

Throughout my childhood, my parents were faced with the unique challenges of raising a child with my condition. Needless to say, supporting their son's effort to write a book was among the most unique. Their encouragement to push ahead with this project and their recollections of my experiences—both good and bad—were very important to me.

Some of my memories of elementary school were a little foggy, but thanks to Bob Gray, I was able to make those moments feel like yesterday. He kept thorough records of all my accomplishments and never threw away of the videotapes of my participation in various activities. Even though it was a little embarrassing to be reminded of myself as an eight-year-old, I'm grateful to Mr. Gray not only for maintaining those videos, but especially for helping to create them, too.

Some members of the Huntingtown High School faculty shared many anecdotes, some of which I was unaware. Mary Casey, Valerie Harrington, Kristin Hunter, Mike Johnson, Sharon Seger, and Dave Taylor all were able to add their invaluable and unique perspective to the experiences I was able to describe in this book. And if Coach Terry Green did not do enough for me already, his diligent record-keeping and videotaping of my matches proved to be excellent resources, as were his memories of our hundreds of hours spent together.

My many friends at Huntingtown, who never backed away from a reporter or cameraman whenever one was at the school to interview me, were just as eager to share their memories of the moments I hold so dearly. Thanks go to Nikki Agambar, Robert Davidson, Katie DeVore, Sean DeVore, Michael Groves, Dusty Jones, Daniel Justice, Jessie Moulton, Brittany Norton, Phil Riley, Kelli Seger, and Curk Smart.

I also want to thank my co-writer, Alan Goldenbach, for his patience with me, as I tried to balance my senior year of high school—the classwork, wrestling, college applications, and general socializing—with this enormous project. I'm grateful to Alan's editors at The Washington Post, particularly Micah Pollack and Jon DeNunzio, for giving him the time to work with me on this book. I'm especially appreciative of Alan's wife, Elyse. She was patient with her husband while he worked with me and also provided important feedback and suggestions for the book's editing, as well as endless support throughout the process.

Alan convinced the people at Sports Publishing, LLC, to believe in my story and consider it worthy of publication. I want to thank Noah Amstadter, Letha Caudill, Andi Hake, Doug Hoepker, Dustin Hubbart, Dave Hulsey, Bob Olson, Jonathan Patterson, and Maurey Williamson, for their tireless work in acquiring, editing, designing, selling, and promoting this book.

I know there are countless others whom I have omitted, but don't think I have forgotten their contributions. It amazes me to have completed this project. I put it right up there with any of my accomplishments on the wrestling mat. It would have been impossible, however, for me to fulfill either effort on my own.

INTRODUCTION

By Alan Goldenbach

Three hours had passed since she had given birth to her fourth child, yet 22-year-old Connie Jenifer had not seen—let alone held—her baby boy. Between the fatigue brought on by the delivery and the sedatives used to ease her through it, Connie drifted in and out of sleep throughout the afternoon of September 7, 1988. When her subconscious finally awoke her for good, it did so with a direct order: Find out where my baby is.

Connie had gone into this pregnancy alone, just as she had done with each of her three prior ones. She had never been married and was used to not having the baby's father beside her in the delivery room. Connie was at the mercy of her parents and four siblings. None of them, though, were in the recovery room at La Plata Hospital in Southern Maryland when Connie awoke. Her instinct told her that something was wrong.

After giving birth earlier in the day, Connie remembered hearing the nurse exclaim, "You have a baby boy." That was perfect. Connie had already picked out a name: Trevon. Now, however, she was worried. "Why can't I see my baby boy?" Connie thought to herself as she lay alone in the recovery room. Charles, one of Connie's two older brothers entered the room with a pale face. Connie's parents followed behind, and stood silently at the doorway as Charles approached Connie's bed. He was as confused as he was upset. Having just returned from active duty in the Marine Corps, Charles thought he would be prepared for the worst. Yet nothing he experienced in his travels to the South Pacific had taught him how to handle a situation like this.

"Where is he already?" Connie asked her brother. "Where is Trevon?"

"Connie," he said, "They're taking him up to Children's Hospital in D.C."

"What?" she asked. "Why?"

"There was a problem," Charles said, adding quickly, "He's going to be all right, but, um, well, they need to run some tests."

"Tests for what?" demanded Connie, who was wide awake by then.

Charles froze, still overcome with shock hours after learning the stunning news. He couldn't spit out the words, despite spending time with his older sister Barbara, rehearsing how to break the news to Connie. He certainly couldn't sugarcoat the message, so he simply told Connie the facts.

"Connie," he said, "your son was born without any legs."

"What?" she asked, more as a threat than a question.

Charles repeated himself, telling Connie that her Trevon was in an ambulance en route to a Children's Hospital about an hour north in Washington, D.C., where tests would be performed to determine if there were any additional birth defects.

"They what?!" she screamed.

Charles put his hand on his sister's shoulder. She tried to swat it away, almost as if to blame her brother for the shocking news. But she was overwhelmed with grief and broke into tears. Shock, sadness, and helplessness attacked Connie from all angles. Having a child with no legs seemed as absurd as having a child with no heart. "Human beings have legs. They all do," she thought. "How can a child with no legs survive? What do I do with a child with no legs? Will he be bedridden his entire life?"

Connie could not comprehend why this birth defect was not detected earlier. She had gone for monthly sonograms beginning in her second trimester. Each time, her doctor told her she was going to have a healthy baby. She later found out that during the seventh month of her pregnancy, her doctor mistook the fetus' arms for its legs when examining the sonogram—news of no condolence to her after the fact.

Connie spent two more days in the hospital before returning home. She lived in her parents' three-bedroom house in La Plata, Maryland, a short drive from Washington D.C. Also living with her parents were two of Connie's children (the third—Latarsha—lived with her father), her younger sister

Tanya, Tanya's husband, and their two children. It was a crowded house, and Connie wanted none of the company when she returned home from the hospital. She locked herself in her bedroom, and, for the next two days, thought only of her predicament—a single, unemployed mother with three children to look after, the youngest of which she thought would require an unfathomable amount of care.

And Connie was the last person to be able to provide that. During her pregnancy, she had heard plenty of criticism from friends and strangers alike about how she shouldn't be having another baby without a husband. La Plata was a small community where everyone knew one another. Gossip spread through the town faster than the flu bug. Now the rumors would only increase. Upon her departure from the hospital, word trickled through La Plata about Connie's newborn boy. Connie was afraid to leave the house and face the concerned looks, the questions, the unwanted advice.

She had quit her job at K-Mart one month prior to giving birth. There was nothing for her to do now but seclude herself, manage her thoughts, and await her son's arrival. Luckily, Connie's baby appeared to be healthy; no further defects were detected. Trevon was ready to come home after a week's worth of tests, but Connie was not ready for him. Deep down, she was terrified to face her new baby for the first time. She had spent the week imagining what a child without legs would look like. Each time she lingered on the thought, she ended up in tears.

Connie's mother, Shirley, and older sister, Barbara, made the hour-long drive to pick Trevon up at the hospital. When they returned, they placed the newborn in the bassinet set up in the living room. Several family members and friends were at the house, each of them more eager to see Trevon than his own mother was. Connie heard the commotion and walked slowly from her bedroom at the rear of the house to the living room in the front, where a couple dozen people awaited her. She looked down into the bassinet and found her baby wrapped in a blanket and sound asleep, just like her three other children were when they had come home from the hospital. She leaned over to pick up her son. As she did, the blanket slid off of Trevon's body, and exposed his lower torso and his missing legs. Connie burst out crying. Charles and Barbara rushed over to hug their sister. Barbara grabbed Trevon, wrapped the blanket around him, and returned him to the bassinet. After rehearsing this moment in her head for a week, Connie was still unprepared for the sight of her baby.

Connie could no longer live in denial, nor could she run away. She had stayed away from the hospital and avoided the public in an attempt to convince herself that a mistake had been made—that this baby boy was not truly hers. But as she looked down at the bassinet, Connie realized she could not avoid dealing with what was lying in front of her.

"Everything is going to be alright," her mother reassured her. "Everything is going to be alright."

"Really?" Connie asked between sobs, almost waiting for her mother to admit she was wrong. "Why me?" she demanded to know. "Why me?"

Shirley spoke the only words that could have lifted Connie's spirits at that moment.

"When the good Lord takes something, he replaces it with something else," she said.

Connie thought about that for a moment. She looked around the room at everyone else, and wondered to herself, "What will my baby have that these people don't?" It wasn't going to be something she could see right away. Connie had to be patient, and at 22 years old, patience was a virtue she had not yet acquired. Reluctantly, she realized it was her only option.

"Okay," Connie told her mother, as she wiped away more tears. "We're going to try this."

Just then, Connie heard a whisper in the room. One of the men asked his wife if Connie was serious. How could she keep this baby? What made Connie think she could care for a baby who needed so much help? She had to give him up for adoption. Or at least put him in the hands of someone who knew how to give him the proper care.

Connie snapped back, suddenly protective of Trevon: "I heard that! This is my child! If the good Lord gave him to me like that, then that's how I'm going to take him."

And with that, Connie asked everyone to leave.

Fear took the place of denial the first two days that Trevon was home. Connie struggled to sleep at night, intimidated by the task at hand. Finally, she confronted the situation the only way she knew: in the middle of the night, she picked Trevon up and brought him into her bedroom. If she was going to raise Trevon, she had to learn to feel comfortable with him. So Connie isolated the two of them in her bedroom. She was lucky enough to have her parents there to tend to her other children. She used the time to look into Trevon's eyes. Hour after hour, Connie said to herself, "I've got to do this myself. I've got to prove I can do it."

For the first month, Connie never left the house, except to take Trevon to the doctor. Isolation proved to be encouraging for her, even as she struggled with the simplest tasks of motherhood. Trevon forced her to relearn several practices that had become routine. How do you hold a baby with no legs? Connie was used to resting the baby's head and back on her left forearm, while cradling the legs in the palm of her right hand. What, now, would she do with her right hand? She couldn't hold Trevon with just one hand. How do you put a diaper on a baby with no legs? How do you secure it so that it doesn't slide off? Connie wasted a couple dozen diapers before she learned how tightly to fasten the adhesive clasps on the sides of the diaper. Eventually, she got it.

A couple weeks into her new life with Trevon, just as she was entering into a comfort zone, Connie received a surprise visitor. It was her friend Reggie, Trevon's father. Connie and Reggie met while they attended La Plata High School. Reggie was a year older, and Connie's crush on him didn't fade, even four years after she graduated. Connie figured their one-night fling was never going to amount to anything more than that. But when she discovered she was pregnant, Connie confronted Reggie and told him the baby was his. He denied it.

As the pregnancy progressed, though, Connie continued to badger Reggie to accept responsibility, and he acquiesced. He began talking to Connie about helping her raise their baby, and Connie was thrilled at the prospect. Finally, one of her children would get the attention and care of two parents, and it would be the one child who needed it the most. Yet Connie wondered where Reggie had been during the past two weeks. He said he didn't know that Connie had given birth, which she knew was a lie, because anyone with an ear in La Plata had heard about Connie's baby. But Connie was desperate for help, and if Reggie was going provide some, she wouldn't harp on a little immaturity.

Connie invited Reggie into the living room to meet Trevon. They walked over to the bassinet, and before Connie could reach down to pick up Trevon, Reggie gasped.

"Are you sure he's mine?" he asked Connie, as he saw Trevon for the first time.

"You're damned right he is," she retorted, with a smile. "Isn't he beautiful?"

But Reggie wasn't joking. He continued to debate whether he could have been the father. He suggested that their night together was longer than nine months ago. Connie insisted he was the only man she had been with during that time. Reggie looked down into the bassinet once more and shook his head. He turned and walked out of the house without saying another word. Once outside, he took off running, away from the house. Connie threw her hands up in the air. "Come back here!" she yelled at him, before she started to cry again. The help she so desperately needed was sprinting down the street—away from her.

Still, Connie persisted, calling Reggie every day for the next few weeks. He never answered. After a month, the number was disconnected. She wrote letters to him as well. After three went unanswered, the fourth came back to Connie's house marked "Return to Sender." Reggie had moved. Connie was a single mother again.

Trevon returned to the hospital for additional tests over the next few months, and luckily, no other birth defects were detected. His vision, hearing, and motor skills were all fine. Yet no one could give Connie an answer as to why Trevon had been born without legs. Doctors told Connie that all birth defects result from both genetic and environmental factors. Connie didn't smoke or drink during the pregnancy. Trevon's condition—congenital amputation, in which a baby is missing all or part of a limb—often occurs in the first few weeks of a pregnancy, before a woman is even aware she is pregnant. The condition is usually undetectable until birth. The exact cause is unknown, but, according to the March of Dimes, it results from a combination of factors, both environmental and genetic. Amputation could follow exposure to a teratogen, an agent—such as a virus, a drug, radiation, or another substance—that interferes with embryonic development. There are additional cases, according to the March of Dimes, in which tight amniotic bands constrict the development of a limb.

This was difficult for Connie to understand, and it bothered her. She needed to know one thing: Was there something wrong with her that caused her baby to not have legs? Did she do something to prompt this biological stutter? Did Reggie do something? Doctors could only give her one answer: it was a freak occurrence. According to the March of Dimes, one out of every 2,000 babies is born without all or part of a limb. But that wasn't a good enough explanation for Connie. Fourteen months after Trevon's birth, she received her answer when she gave birth to her fifth child, Jamar. He was born with two legs and a healthy body; finally, she could accept that what had happened to Trevon was just as the doctors had suggested. Connie was relieved that the problem was not inherent to her.

Six months after Jamar's birth, Connie again became overwhelmed by the community's gossip and continual judgment of her. She worried about how Trevon would be received in the community once he was old enough to understand the gossip, which she was hearing even in her parents' own home. She decided it was time to get her own place.

"I need to move out," Connie told her parents. "I got myself into this, and I've got to get myself out of it. You aren't always going to be there for me."

Shirley didn't want Connie to leave. Her daughter was vulnerable and angry, and Shirley worried that Connie had made a decision based more upon emotion than reason. She convinced Connie to leave her two older sons, nine-year-old Paul and eight-year-old Marcus, with her in La Plata. They were already in school there and had established friends in the community.

Connie packed up her car and took Trevon, three months shy of his third birthday, and Jamar, who was six months old, north to Suitland, a black community just over the Maryland border with Washington, D.C. Connie knew she could blend in there more easily due to the denser population. Nobody knew her there, and Connie just wanted to fade into the background. She went to the Tooley Street Station apartment complex, and the landlord suggested she move into a two-bedroom unit with another woman who had two young children of her own. The woman's roommate had just moved out, and since Connie was still unemployed, she was looking to save money on rent. This was a cheaper option than having her own place, so Connie happily agreed.

For the first time in her life, Connie was on her own. For all the bravado with which she prided herself by eschewing the crutch of her parents' care and home, Connie wondered if she had made another bad choice. She had no job, two young boys to care for, and was an hour's drive from the only people and life she knew. She was lonely, and she was scared.

Flanked by four of his buddies, Eric Brown was walking down Parkway Terrace Drive on a Saturday night with a bottle of beer n his hand, trying his best to mind his own business. You never had to go far to find trouble in Suitland, Maryland. Even though it sits just over Washington, D.C.'s southeast border with Maryland,

Suitland's identity lies close to the heart of Prince George's County. In 1991, Prince George's surpassed its previous high for murders, the watermark of its escalating rate of violent crime. Eric, who was 23 years old at the time, did not pad those figures. But his four friends—each about three or four years younger than he was—had already had several run-ins with the law.

In fact, Eric was not doing much in the days leading up to September 28, 1991. Less than two months earlier, he was a passenger in his friend's car when they were hit from behind by another car. Eric sustained back and neck injuries, which forced him to leave his job at a nearby liquor store. By the time Eric was ready to go back to work a few weeks later, he learned his job had been permanently filled.

On nights like this, Eric took it upon himself to help keep his younger friends on the straight and narrow. When one of them suggested something unseemly, Eric provided a voice of maturity. But what happened when Eric, himself, was tempted to veer off course? At around nine o'clock that night, that question was put to the test.

"Can I have some of that beer?" said the sweet voice of a woman, coming from a first-floor apartment window. Eric quickly turned his head and was startled, but for a good reason. This wasn't the kind of trouble he thought he'd find. Connie Jenifer was hitting on Eric.

Trouble never came to Eric in such a lovely package. Even though Connie grew up on the fringes of the D.C. area, she had a smooth Southern drawl reminiscent of the girls Eric knew from growing up in a small mining town in southern Virginia. He occasionally dreamed about moving back to that rural community, and, for a moment, his ears had just taken him there. His eyes, meantime, went straight for Connie's. She had big, bright, wide eyes that glowed in the twilight. Eric was mesmerized. "I'll be back," he told his friends, as he strutted over to the window. "Y'all go ahead. I'll catch up with you later."

After a few minutes of small talk, Connie invited Eric to come inside. Connie was embarrassed by her sparsely furnished apartment and the couple with whom she lived. It was hardly a noteworthy first impression. But Eric didn't mind; he was just happy to have run into the right kind of trouble. Connie invited Eric to sit next to her on the sofa in the living room. They started talking about their childhoods, their friends, and their hopes for a better and more stable future. The conversation lasted for more than an hour. All the while, Connie kept her biggest secret to herself. She knew she had a tale to trump all others. Sometimes when she told it people were shocked. Others were amazed. A few cried. But everyone was moved by it.

It took a lot of courage, though, for Connie to tell this particular story, especially to a guy. Finally, though, she mustered the strength to tell it. She had finished sizing up Eric, and saw a softness in him that most 23-year-olds would be mortified to show. Nevertheless, she still feared Eric's reaction to Trevon. Her baby boy was the one topic Connie knew killed potential relationships. Who wanted to be with a single mom? What man would want to help raise a kid who wasn't even his, let alone a kid with no legs?

But as she began to tell the story, Connie noticed that Eric was different. He didn't recoil in horror. He didn't start nudging himself off the couch. He didn't suddenly remember his friends were waiting for him outside. Instead, Eric stayed and listened. After hearing Connie share her story of Trevon, Eric actually wanted to know more. The topic of Trevon did not silence him; in fact, it opened him up more. Each time Connie said something about Trevon, Eric wanted a better description. "Tell me more about the pregnancy," he asked. "Did he have to go through any corrective surgery?" Connie was stunned. "Most of the guys just cut the conversations right there," she recalled years later, "and I never saw them again. Eric understood how hard it was for me."

They spent the night talking, and Connie tried to answer all of Eric's questions. She was able to learn a tidbit or two of her own, about Eric's two daughters, Brittany and Keisha, both of whom lived with their mothers but still saw plenty of their father. Eric was about to see plenty of Trevon. The toddler entered the living room and introduced himself to the new man sitting on the couch. Eric struggled to pay attention to the three-year-old's words; he was captivated by how the kid moved around. The two played on the floor for a bit before Eric had to leave. But Connie wasn't worried. "I had a feeling he might be back," she recalled. Sure, enough, Eric returned within a day. And the next weekend, he was back again. When he showed up at Connie's front door on a Friday night, she confided in him, "I thought you'd be gone like the rest of them."

But Eric wasn't going anywhere. He spent the weekend with the woman and the young boy who would shape the rest of his life.

Eric started to spend more and more time at Connie's apartment over the next few weeks. After a month, he was there more often than he was at his own place. By November, Connie had decided that Eric should move in, and he agreed. There was no sense in them each paying rent, especially after Eric had found a job with a courier service. They weren't talking about marriage just yet. Both Connie and Eric knew they needed stability independently before they could move forward together.

Shortly after moving in, Eric began to notice the impact of Connie's roommates, who had developed a crippling drug addiction. The couple had not paid rent for either of the first two months Eric lived in the building, and they were seldom at the apartment. Eric explained the problem to the landlord, and he told Eric that it was within the tenant's rights to kick the couple out of the apartment if they continued to avoid paying rent.

That was all Eric needed to hear. He went back to the apartment and packed up all of their belongings, placing them in a corner of the living room. He did this reluctantly; Connie had talked him out of putting all of their possessions out on the sidewalk. When one of the roommates came home the following day to find his clothes stuffed into a box, he knew not to belabor the point. He picked up the box and left. It was the last time Connie and Eric saw either of them.

Eric's relationship with Trevon began to blossom. He bought Trevon a Tonka dump truck for Christmas, which Trevon quickly learned was more than just a toy. He liked to squeeze his body into the bed of the truck and push himself around the apartment and outside in the street. Trevon loved to test how fast he could go, but Eric always made sure the boy stayed under control. Trevon trusted Eric. This new man in the house was not a threat to him. He was a friend.

Eric was the first person, aside from Connie, not to baby Trevon. Once he saw Trevon succeed at something, Eric never offered to help him. He watched the three-year-old move around the apartment just as easily as he pulled his toys off a shelf. Trevon could run from one side of the room to the other as fast as anyone his age; he just did it differently. He jumped up and down on his bed as many toddlers do, all the while hoping to touch the ceiling. Whenever Eric looked into Trevon's eyes, he never saw the need for sympathy. He saw an independent kid who was a fast learner—a kid who didn't look to others for help. "So I wasn't going to give him any," Eric said.

Later that spring, on a lazy Saturday afternoon, Eric and Connie babysat twin girls who lived in an upstairs apartment. Trevon and Jamar played on the living room floor, while the two girls sat on the couch behind them and watched television. Trevon and the twin girls were all in the midst of potty training, but the girls were making an easier adjustment. Trevon was too old for a diaper by then, but Connie and Eric still put one on him. It was difficult, though, for Trevon to move around on his hands without the diaper shifting or falling off altogether, so he often slid out of the diaper when he was home, especially when it was bedtime. Despite the potty training, and Connie and Eric often had to clean up the floor after him.

With four kids under the age of four in the apartment that afternoon, Connie and Eric hardly had time to relax. Whether it was Trevon chasing Jamar across the apartment, or one of the girls asking for something to eat, Connie and Eric were on their feet the whole day. Finally, when they had some quiet, they sat down on their bed and turned on the television. An intriguing sound ended five minutes of peace: the toilet flushed. From their bed, Connie and Eric looked into the living room, where Jamar and the two girls played quietly. Eric looked over at Connie and asked, "Who's in the bathroom?"

Connie got up and could not believe what she saw. Trevon had used the toilet, as if he had been doing it every day of his life. Connie watched him lower the seat, leap on top of it, and, from there, boost himself onto the sink to wash his hands. Then, Trevon lowered himself onto the floor. Connie reached for the towel against the back of the door to hand it to Trevon, but her son snatched it before she could.

"I got it," he told her, a sign of how he would decline help at every turn.

By that time, Eric joined Connie in doorway. They stood silently in stunned disbelief. Trevon scooted right past them, heading back into the living room to play with his brother.

"I was worried that he was going to fall," Eric recalled. "He just came out like he did it all the time. He wasn't smiling. He wasn't looking for us to congratulate him."

That was okay, because Eric was speechless. At that moment, Eric saw the two qualities that would come to define this unique boy—determination and fearlessness.

Oh, the potential, Eric thought.

1

I spend my life walking on my hands. So, when people tell me I do crazy things with my body, I just laugh. But even I had to admit that I went too far this time. Wrestling? This had to be the craziest thing I'd ever done. What was I trying to prove? What did I need to prove? Surely I'd proven enough already.

I was born without any legs, a condition called congenital amputation, in which a newborn is missing all or part of a limb. Some babies are missing a finger. Some are missing an arm or a leg. My body ends at my hip sockets. I don't even have a stub of a leg. My body is only 2 feet 11 inches tall, and I weigh about 105 pounds. My wingspan is 6 feet, 4 inches, so that gives me an idea of how tall I'd be if I had legs—probably over 6 feet tall. But I don't spend much time wondering, "What it?" To get around, my arms have to function as legs. I plant the palms of my hands on the ground, and pull my torso forward like a swing.

I've surprised a lot of people with how quickly I've learned to move about. I can run laps around a track, and do pushups and jumping jacks about twice as quickly as anyone else, because I only have half the body to elevate. If I need to boost myself up into a chair, I use one hand to lift myself off of the ground, and the other to grab on to the seat. If I need to open a door, I grab the handle and either pull or push the door out, and use my other hand to pivot my body around the door's edge.

By using my arms as my means of transportation, I've built up some pretty impressive upper-body strength. I developed muscles in parts of my hands and arms that most people don't even realize they have. For example, my hands are enormous: my wrist to the tip of my middle finger measures almost nine inches. My fingers are very loose and dexterous, and I have broad shoulders and toned forearms. This specialized strength allowed me to thrive in wheelchair athletics, particularly track events. I started competing for a Washington, D.C.-based team when I was five years old, and by the time I was eight, I had set junior national records in the 100-, 200- and 400-meter races—marks that still stand ten years later. These records are categorized according to disability, as well as age. When I raced, I sometimes competed against—and dominated—teenagers, well before my 10th birthday.

If that's not impressive enough, I accomplished this despite growing up in poverty in one of the nastiest ghettos in Maryland, just over the Washington, D.C. border. I can't even count the number of times I awoke in the middle of the night and had to roll out of bed to take cover on the floor because I heard gunshots fired right outside my house. While watching TV in the living room, my parents often had to crank the volume on the set to drown out the police sirens blaring outside. On a regular basis, I witnessed car chases, drug deals gone bad, and crooks running through the woods that lined the dead-end street on which we lived.

A lot of people told me that it was a miracle I made it to my teenage years, regardless of my disability. It wasn't because of anything I did. I knew that the longer I was in such a dangerous environment, the better the chances were that bad luck would catch up to me. On any given day, I could have been in the wrong place at the wrong time, and—boom!—my life would be over. Yet I survived.

Midway through my junior year of high school, I was at a new school in a new home, far away from the gunshots and the screeching tires. My family moved out of the ghetto to a developing suburb in Maryland. I was passing my classes, making friends with people I thought I had nothing in common with, and doing things people said I had no business doing. I was learning to adapt, and proving people wrong in the process.

I love to smile, and everyone who met me at my new school thought I was "the cutest little thing." My new classmates and teachers would give me an affectionate pat on the shoulder, and tell me how I amazed them. Maybe my smile invited those compliments, but I couldn't stand them nonetheless. Sure, it was always nice to hear a kind word or two. What people never understood about me, though, was that I never saw myself as being any different from anyone else.

That probably sounds like the craziest idea I've ever had—sillier than trying to wrestle or walking on my hands, thinking I could blend in with everyone else. Trust me, though. I know crazy, and this isn't it. I know people are stunned to see me mosey into a room with no legs, and wonder how I get around. They think I don't know what it's like to run, walk, or jump, so I must be different. They realize I am incapable of something as basic as carrying an object, because I need to use both hands in order to walk. There isn't anyone like me at their school, their church, or their office. They've never seen anyone like me on the street. I know how people react to me: I watch peoples' eyes and mouths every day.

But what people never seemed to grasp—even after the novelty fades of seeing someone like me walking around with no legs—is that I see that person every day when I look in the mirror. I've seen that same image since I was born in 1988. I never did a double take when I saw that person, nor did I think twice about treating him differently than others. I never saw vulnerability or helplessness in his eyes. I didn't see somebody looking for sympathy. Instead, I saw somebody determined to prove that he belongs with people who think he doesn't fit in.

And that was a big part of why I wanted to wrestle. It's a sport where you have no one to look to but yourself. All of your success can be attributed to you—your skills, your work ethic, your determination. So, too, can your failures. Wrestling was a brand-new challenge for me. But at the same time, I hoped that it would prove to be a way in, another tool that I could use to adapt to my surroundings and blend in.

I might have been the most driven teenager in my school, but I couldn't wrestle a dummy when I arrived at Huntingtown High School in an outer Maryland suburb of Washington, D.C. in fall 2004. I thought a good way to make friends in a new community was to join a high school sports team, and serve as a team manager. So I considered my options. But my stepfather suggested instead of being a manager, that I should try out for a sport. He had wrestled in high school and enjoyed it, so he suggested I think about wrestling. I had never wrestled in my life—not counting playing with my younger brother—but I gave it a shot.

Sixty-seven seconds after the opening whistle of my first regular-season match, I was pinned. My opponent from Lackey High School watched me dance around for a while, but I was being silly. I tried to give the impression that I was waiting to make my move. I remembered watching old clips of Muhammad Ali— "float like a butterfly, sting like a bee." I tried to replicate Ali on the wrestling mat, only I didn't pack much sting at all. I wasn't aggressive. I was afraid to attack my opponent, so I just moved around the mat.

Eventually, he took one step, dropped me backwards, and before I knew it, the referee slapped the mat to end the match. He had me on my back, and I was dead. I couldn't get up off my back like most people can—by pushing off the ground with their hands and feet. My opponent had my arms down, and I don't have feet with which to push off. I had no idea what I was doing out there. At that time, I only weighed 95 pounds, while my opponents were as heavy as 105; I was sacrificing 10 percent of my body weight in a sport where weight dictates a level playing field. But I hadn't realized that yet. I just figured I had to go out there, grab on to my opponent, and push him over. Boy, was I wrong.

Not for a second, though, did I think this was funny. I felt like I had cheated the rest of the team by giving such a poor showing of myself. The pin cost my team six points in the match. I only thought about that, while I sat on the bench and watched the rest of my teammates wrestle that night. Throughout the preseason, they took the time to teach me the sport, and by the time the regular season started, they told me they thought I could win. I had let them down.

I thought back to my success in wheelchair track, and how easily that sport came to me. Throughout my life, once I had figured out the sport, I then dominated. When I won races, I blew away the field. I certainly wasn't used to losing, and I didn't like it one bit. Not only did I lose my first wrestling match, but also this time, I was the one being dominated. It was the first time I felt I had truly failed in a sport, and it worried me what its impact would have on my teammates.

Our team captain was Phil Riley, a heavyweight wrestler. He ended his wrestling career later that season with a state championship and went on to sign a football scholarship with Hofstra. I looked up to Phil as a big brother; if I wanted to learn this sport,

I wanted to learn it from the best. Right after I lost, I went off behind the team bench, and sat alone against the wall to sulk. Phil was the first guy on the team to come up to me, look me in the eyes, and say, "Don't you give up." That meant so much to me. The captain believed in me.

At the same time, though, there was this other feeling that pierced my insides with fear and doubt. What if Phil was just being nice? What if he and the rest of my teammates were just giving me the same kind—but ultimately hollow—words of encouragement I had grown accustomed to from strangers? Deep down, were they bitter about having me on their team? At the end of each excruciating, three-hour practice, did they look over at me and think, "Well, there goes our chance this season. Trevon, the cripple, is going to get whooped each time, and cost our team points"? What if they were waiting for the first match to see if their thoughts would be confirmed?

During the three days in between that first match and my next one, I thought about the task in front of me: proving to my teammates—and myself—that I belonged. Dealing with that pressure wasn't easy, and one night, when I could not fall asleep, I lay in bed and asked myself some serious questions: What am I getting myself into? Is it worth the humiliation? Should I just quit now? I knew that would save me from more embarrassment and my teammates from more disappointment. But to quit was not in my nature. That would have been what everyone expected of me. It would have been another way for people to give me more of those kind gestures, telling me how proud they were of me for just trying. I didn't want to just try. I made the decision to play this sport, and I was going to see it through. It didn't matter if I lost every match. I told myself that I had to complete a high school wrestling season. In order to do that, I had to prove to my teammates that I deserved to be on their team. Getting pinned was no way to do that.

I didn't have to pump myself up for our next match against Eleanor Roosevelt High. This was our first home meet of the year, and it was my chance to erase the first impression I left on my teammates three days earlier. I was surprised when a couple hundred people showed up to cheer us on—a large crowd for a Tuesday night high school wrestling match. But as I later found out, high school wrestling is very popular in Calvert County, where my new high school resided. Fans know good wrestling when they see it, and I was sure more than a few of them thought I was a gimmick.

One of the first lessons my stepfather taught me about wrestling was about giving a first impression to your opponent that would work to your advantage. I was determined to do so before this match. When schools have dual meets—one school's team of wrestlers against another's—the lineups are introduced before the first match. Each team's wrestler is called out to the center of the mat, shakes hands with his opponent, and then retreats to the sideline with the rest of his teammates. My stepfather suggested that when I shake my opponent's hand during the introductions, I should give a really limp grip. He thought that would make my opponent question my toughness. From the moment my opponent shakes my hand until the match starts, he will be thinking that I'm going to be easy to defeat.

My father suggested that when I step onto the mat to begin my match, and the referee asks both wrestlers to shake hands again, I should then give him a very firm grip. Suddenly, my opponent's mind will be distracted, thinking about that handshake. "What happened to that limp-wristed guy I shook hands with earlier?" he'll wonder.

Since I was wrestling in the 103-pound weight class—the lightest in the state—most of my opponents were freshmen and sophomores. Not only were these the smallest wrestlers, most of them were young kids, and I could intimidate them easily and get inside their heads. Hopefully, after that handshake, my opponent would spend the first few seconds of the match in a timid state of confusion. Without any legs, I was starting every match at a disadvantage. This was one way I could begin to even the score.

Sure enough, when the match was about to begin, I gave my opponent such a firm handshake that I knew he was surprised. When the referee dropped his right arm to start the match, I didn't dance around like I had done in my first match. I went straight for his right leg. Within 15 seconds, I had scored a two-point takedown. I felt myself moving around a lot easier, and with a lot more command. Near the end of the first period, he and I were locked into a clench near the edge of the circle. Suddenly, he had me on my back, and for a second I thought things were going to end just as they did in my first match. It was less than two minutes in, and I was in prime position to get pinned, even though I was ahead on points, 4-3.

For the first time in my young wrestling career, I learned how quickly wrestlers have to think—and act. I had room to move my left arm, so I used it to slide out of his grasp, and in one fluid motion, flip him over and out of bounds. That stopped the action for a moment, and as I lay there, I thought about how lucky I was to have escaped a pin and regained control of the match.

I started the second period just like the first; I grabbed my opponent's right leg, spun him around, and earned another two-point takedown within 20 seconds. That put me up 6-3 in points. A reversal about 30 seconds later gave me an 8-3 advantage. And with that reversal, I put him on his back. Another first-time emotion swept over me: I was in total control. I had his left shoulder blade totally pinned, so I maneuvered to get his right one down and finish him off. Believe it or not, the last thing on my mind was, "Oh my God, I'm going to pin a guy." Rather, at that moment I thought what his next move would be. In practice, when I had guys in this position, they had an easy move— bridge their body by planting their feet down, lifting their torso off of the ground, and in the process flipping me off of them onto my back. Other wrestlers can stop this move by using their own legs to tie up those of their opponents'. Of course, that wasn't an option for me.

Out of the corner of my eye, I saw his right knee bend. He was starting to make that move, and that got me worried. I couldn't blow this one. After losing my first match by a quick pin, I couldn't lose my second match when it appeared like I had it in the bag. I had to stop that leg from moving any further, so I kept his left shoulder down with my right arm, and slid my left arm down to his lower leg. I figured if I could flatten out his leg, his back would drop squarely on the mat.

His foot moved a lot easier than I thought it would, sort of sliding along the mat without much resistance. When his back hit the mat as expected, I still didn't feel like I had him. Even with the fans screaming, the referee leaning in so close that I could smell his breath, and my opponent struggling to break free, I didn't realize that I was on the verge of a pin. I was so focused on what could happen next, that I didn't even savor the moment. One of the first things I learned from my teammates was to always think a couple of moves ahead. I had to assume my opponent would get out of this. What move would he make?

My thought was cut short as the referee's palm slapped the mat. BAM! I had pinned my opponent, and the crowd went berserk. I rolled off of my opponent and onto my back, and shut my eyes for a couple of seconds. I was too tired to think about what I had just accomplished. I just needed to zone out for a moment.

I gathered myself and headed to the middle of the mat to shake my opponent's hand, as the referee raised my left arm. At that moment, I looked around the gym—at my parents, teammates, coaches, and the fans. I saw a lot people with tears in their eyes. This never happened at a wheelchair track meet. I was taken aback.

Back at my team's bench, my coaches were all ready to congratulate me. But before they could, Dusty Jones, our 171-pounder and a co-captain, picked me up and carried me around the sideline, so I could high-five each of my teammates. That was the biggest surprise of the night—the one thing I'll never forget about my first victory in wrestling. That move by Dusty signified that I belonged with my teammates. I owed them a victory after how poorly I had wrestled three days earlier against Lackey, and this was vindication for me.

As we watched the final match of the night—the crowd still abuzz after my victory—I pondered on what I had accomplished with that victory. I had set so many goals when I decided to wrestle, and I thought about two of them that were accomplished in one night: to get a victory, and to get a pin. But I had also shown that I had the potential to do a lot more. It occurred to me right then that wrestling could open a lot of doors for me—athletically, academically, and socially.

Afterward, the entire team decided to meet up at Ruby Tuesdays, a restaurant down the road from our high school. That became our routine after every home meet. I got into Phil Riley's truck, and on the 10-minute drive to the restaurant, I thought some more about the night. I had never experienced this kind of emotion and intensity in wheelchair track. There was never this kind of fan interest or camaraderie with my teammates. When we got to the restaurant, our team sat at a long table in the back. We didn't talk at all about wrestling or even my own surprising victory. Instead the conversation centered on typical things that concerned high school boys: girlfriends, anxiety over getting a drivers' license, installing a new car stereo. In a word, it was normal.

It didn't matter that I was the only black kid surrounded by white kids whom I had met just three months earlier. It didn't matter that I was the only kid at the table without legs. I felt completely at ease with my teammates. I was a part of something that I believed was important, and everyone else there shared that sentiment. This was a feeling—a bond—that was often absent in other areas of my life. I didn't know what it was like to share my emotions with teammates—with friends—until that night. When wheelchair track meets ended, the conversations still revolved around competition. The track meets controlled my life, and even if I wanted to escape that, my coaches wouldn't let me. We were all so passionate about succeeding at the meets that we never discussed life outside of competition. My wrestling teammates were passionate about their sport, too, but they genuinely cared about each other's lives off of the mat as well.

After about an hour or so at the restaurant, Phil drove me home. I went into my bedroom and looked at the bookcase where I displayed some of my trophies, medals, and award certificates from wheelchair sports. There were about three dozen items on the shelves, and about twice that many stored away in my closet. This was what I would point to as proof of my success—but others couldn't relate to wheelchair sports.

Now, just from that one evening, I saw a glimpse of what the wrestling community could provide for me. I could finally be a part of a traditional sport. I was shut out my entire childhood from playing basketball, football, or baseball with other kids my age. I had to play with other disabled people. Because I never saw myself as being different, I never wanted to play with people who needed to be treated differently. As I sat in that restaurant with my new teammates, I saw the friendships that this sport could provide for me. I'd had close friendships before, but never with teammates, who have a special kind of closeness due to the field of competition.

As I lay in bed that night, I thought about the attention paid to this sport by the crowd that night, and then I thought about the eyes and mouths of the people I encounter every day. I considered how I could use this attention to my advantage, and achieve an ultimate goal—helping people. I'd been helped so many times by so many people during my childhood. Eventually, I knew my turn would come to return the favor and help people on my own.

My mother reminded me throughout my childhood: "Trevon, God put you on this Earth to do something to inspire people. When you inspire people, you help them to do better things."

Finally, I had figured out how I would inspire people and repay the debt: wrestling.

2

Even after three years of raising a child with no legs, my mother still looked at me in disbelief every so often. I was always very outgoing and adventurous as a child. I never hesitated to try something new, whether it was playing with a new toy, climbing on the furniture at my grandmother's house, or bounding out the door to play outside. I didn't see myself as being at a disadvantage simply because I lacked legs. But for my mother, it wasn't so simple.

She had a tough time taking me outside in public. She was emotionally scarred by the rumors and gossip spread around the La Plata community when I was born. Those words about her being an irresponsible mother—and someone incapable of raising a child who needed extra care—remained with her in the back of her mind, no matter how much time she spent with me, and watched me grow up healthy and capable. Despite her wounds, however, I never had any doubt that she loved me. In fact, she was always so proud of me because I never felt sorry for myself, nor did I withdraw and keep to myself. I owe her for the fact that there's usually a smile on my face.

My appearance never embarrassed my mother, but it became tedious for her to share my story with every stranger who saw me for the first time and was naturally curious. I looked different, and there had to be an explanation why. Of course, what angered my mother the most was that there was no concrete explanation. I was just a freak of nature, and that was the reason she gave to anyone who asked. Half of them believed her; but the other half rolled their eyes, thinking that was a line she made up. She was obviously a woman in denial, they thought. Her baby had to have something seriously wrong with him. Or maybe something was wrong with her and she didn't want to admit it.

If she had carried around my medical records, she could have slammed the proof in their faces. I visited doctors several times over my first few years. They made sure I had no other developmental setbacks. I just didn't have any legs. But that was about to change. When I was four years old, it became apparent that the rest of my body would grow normally. My head, arms, and torso were in correct proportion to one another, and I didn't lack any strength. My motor and neurological skills were normal. My mother and my doctor, Dr. Charles Epps at D.C. General Hospital, talked for several months about fitting me with prosthetic legs. Dr. Epps referred me to a doctor in Prince George's County, Dr.

Herbert Goller, who made my prosthesis, and repaired it for me when I grew and needed to have it adjusted.

My new legs weren't functional, just cosmetic. They would, however, make me look a lot like everyone else—except of course for the fact that I would be confined to a wheelchair, which I had already learned to use at this young age. These legs would be my disguise. I was able to ride around, and look like any other person in a wheelchair. That seldom attracted any attention. People were used to seeing someone—even as young as I was—riding in a wheelchair. That saved my mother and me from many random conversations with curious strangers.

The prosthetic legs were attached to a plastic hip socket, which I called a bucket. I sat in the bucket and fastened a strap-like belt around my stomach to secure it to my body. The device allowed me to stand up—and even move around—as long as I had something to lean on. Initially, I used a walker, but as I got older, I learned to use crutches, but those were very difficult. Anytime I stood up, it felt like I was on stilts, so when-ever I had my legs on, I usually remained in my wheelchair or a regular chair.

Before I first stood up on my new legs, I had to learn how to balance my body. I've seen other four-year-olds—with real legs—have trouble maintaining their balance. It was a hundred times harder for me when I was that age and had just been given these new legs. The first time I wore them, I wasn't particularly excited about having a higher vantage point when I stood up. Instead, I was more concerned with being able to manipulate the legs. The easy part was putting them on. It was a challenge trying to move them with my body attached.

There were locks in the prosthesis where the body's joints were supposed to be—at the hips and knees. The locks were there to stabilize the device when I stood up, and allow it to bend when I sat down. It worked a lot like the human body, where joints locked in order to give support and firmness. I turned these locks by pulling on a short cord inside the socket, but it took me a while to get comfortable with that. I had to reach into the bucket, underneath my body, in order to grab the cord.

I liked to wear the device because it helped me blend in a little better. Whenever I went out of the house in public, my parents usually told me to wear it. For example, if we went to the mall or the movies, I was "in my legs." But if we just went to visit my grandmother, my parents would let me go out on my hands. I just had to be careful. My stepfather warned me at a young age that I had to be especially careful of the ground because of the neighborhood where we lived. The streets weren't safe for kids— especially a kid who walked on his hands and had to be wary of broken glass and other sharp debris. And, of course, people didn't clean up after their dogs on my street. That was a nasty obstacle, which, luckily, I always avoided. I would have never heard the end of it from my parents if I had come home with dog doo on my hands. They never would have let me out of my legs again.

So the legs worked to my benefit when I was a young child. But once I started growing, the legs became more difficult to wear. As my body grew, I needed to go to Dr. Goller to get the bucket reshaped. That usually happened every year or so, because that was as often as our insurance provider would cover the expenses. But once I hit my growth spurt, I started growing too quickly for those annual remodelings. Eventually I had to squeeze my body into the bucket, which was too small for me, and it started to pinch the bottom of my torso. I was always energetic, and the prosthesis constricted me, so I usually took it off as soon as I got home. Eventually I got into the habit of not wanting to wear it, and my parents didn't like that. Soon, the legs became more of an annoyance for me, and I was ready to leave them behind.

My attitude toward my fake legs probably began to change shortly after I began attending school. I started at James Ryder Randall Elementary School when I was in kindergarten in 1993. My zoned school was only about a mile away from where I lived, but I went to Randall instead, even though it was about a half-hour away by bus. I attended Randall because it was the only school in Maryland to have an extensive program for children with special needs—physical, emotional, or academic. It was a good environment for me because it helped me understand that there were other children with developmental disabilities. At Randall, I encountered classmates with a great variety of difficulties. There were common handicaps like hearing, speech, and emotional, but there were also more complex issues, such as neuromuscular and orthopedic conditions like spina bifida or multiple sclerosis. I usually had no more than a dozen classmates, and rarely were any two students of equal ability. Almost each student was able to do something very well—sometimes better than anyone else in the class—but that same student was also incapable of doing at least something that nearly everyone else could. I learned a very mature lesson at a young age—humility. And that was tough, because I was one of the most outspoken and active kids in my class. I was proud to show off what I could do.

It was important for me to enjoy school and use it as an outlet for my social and athletic development. My neighborhood was not a safe place to play, so I had to take advantage of what school had to offer. Our apartment in Suitland was part of a huge complex of nondescript red-brick apartments called Tooley Street Station. There were dozens of three-story buildings in the development, which was located a block off Suitland Parkway, a major thoroughfare that connects Prince George's County to the Southeast quadrant of Washington, D.C. There was very little scenery in my neighborhood. Each set of buildings had a parking lot that ate up any grass that I could have played on, and across the street were a couple of abandoned homes and a vacant field littered with debris. School was my safe haven and my playground.

When I was in kindergarten, Mrs. Reeves, the head of the special education wing, saw me scooting through the hallway on my hands and told me to stop. I thought she was going to tell me to put my legs back on, but instead she introduced me to a man who was going to be my physical education teacher the following school year. Bob Gray knelt down on the floor and shook my hand. I looked him over, and immediately noticed his white hair and kind smile. I didn't think much about meeting him at the time. I said, "Hey there," and scooted off. Little did I know how important Mr. Gray would become to me later on.

Mr. Gray had traveled across the country, teaching physical education at schools from the Midwest to the Pacific Coast while dreaming of becoming a basketball coach. He had grown up in rural Indiana, where basketball was every kid's passion. In 1985, he took a job at Oxon Hill Elementary School in Prince George's County, and there he began working with special education students for the first time. He loved it, as the job allowed him to utilize his tremendous creativity, which was essential in devising unique ways to motivate disabled children and keep them active. He loved building weird contraptions suited to a kid's unique disability, which would allow the child to be able to do a particular activity.

Mr. Gray cared the most about getting results, not filling out all of the paperwork that proved he was a great teacher. That was particularly important when teaching special education students; most of the time, it is impossible to chronicle our development in hard and fast terms. Sometimes it was impractical to describe the development of a student's abilities in just words or numbers. Mr. Gray always felt that seeing the action and the student's emotion provided all the necessary documentation. If only he could have been my math teacher, too.

The school bureaucracy, though, started to weigh on him after a few years. After six years at Oxon Hill, he took a year off and contemplated moving again or leaving the education field altogether. When a friend told him about a job vacancy at Randall, Mr. Gray was skeptical. But when his friend told him, "You'll think you have died and gone to heaven when you get to Randall," Mr. Gray gave it a shot.

He came by Randall in spring 1992 to see the school's physical education department in action. Mr. Gray approached physical education with the idea that kids needed to be aerobically fit. He wanted to see what kind of activities the staff did to motivate the children to stay active. What he saw appalled him. On one particular day, the children who used crutches, walkers, or wheelchairs competed in a cross-country race. There was a 600-meter course set up on the school grounds, and teachers were assigned to help some of the children who needed it most. It wasn't really a competition, but just a way for the kids to be active outdoors. Instead, it turned into a competition between the adults. One woman dragged a girl in a walker so hard that the girl fell down several times. A couple of men pushed students in wheelchairs so fast that not only did the students not use their arms to push the wheels, but they were scared they might fall out of the chairs.

Mr. Gray quickly established his first rule change for the following year: adults were not allowed to help the children to this degree. There was no physical benefit for the children when the teacher was the one expending all of the energy and effort. Mr. Gray wanted children to learn at a young age the value of being active and independent. He wanted to see the kids put forth the effort.

I remember one kid in my class named Nick, who was in a wheelchair with a severe spinal disability. He could barely lift anything, let alone a basketball. Mr. Gray attached a basketball to a heavy string for Nick. Then he lowered the basketball hoop to where it was about at eye level with Nick in his wheelchair. Mr. Gray then asked Nick to try to put the ball into the basket. The first time, it took Nick about a minute to do it once. By the end of the school year, however, Nick was making 20 shots in a minute, and we could all see how proud it made him. These were the stories that made Mr. Gray the happiest.

The only times I ever saw him get upset or angry were when students approached an activity with a fear of failure. Mr. Gray wanted everyone to try things. He saw we were limited, and he worried that our disabilities would inhibit us from staying active. So he urged us to expand our options for physical activity. That's why he and I got along so well. He always tried to come up with new things to do, and I was willing to try anything. He challenged me, and I embraced the challenge.

One day, though, he saw me climbing on a side horse, the kind that's used in gymnastics. I knew nothing about this equipment; I just saw it as a new place for me to explore. I loved shuffling along the balance beam on my hands, and plopping onto the cushy mats. By the time I was eight, Mr. Gray decided to teach me moves on the apparatus. He taught me how to walk on my hands the way two-legged people do, inverting my body to where the bottom of my torso pointed skyward. After I mastered that on the mat, I learned how to do it on the narrow balance beam. Eventually, Mr. Gray and I would race each other along the mat in front of the rest of the class.

I liked climbing on the side horse and balance beam because they both allowed me to suspend my body off the ground. I created this one move that was very popular in the class, and, of course, I named it after myself—"The Trey." I rotated my hips, much like Olympic gymnasts would, while moving my body with my hands from one end of the side horse to the other. Each time I lifted a hand to move my body, I swung my hips to that side. When I got to the end of the horse, I would lift my body up into a handstand and then vault off of the beam in a somersault. It took me a while to perfect this move, but Mr. Gray had a video camera and recorded me trying to do this several times during my third grade year. It was amazing how much more at ease I appeared in April compared to February. Earlier, I was hesitant to make each move, and I often slipped off of the apparatus. But by springtime, I would have scored a perfect 10 if this were an Olympic event.

Mr. Gray didn't limit us to obscure sports that none of us had ever seen before. He knew that we wondered what it was like to play the traditional sports that we saw our friends play or watched on television. He set up softball games, where we would hit off of a tee. We all played in the field, and I loved to do that. It allowed me to get out of my prosthesis and run around the field.

We tried sports I would have never thought about playing. The most unbelievable one was soccer. Here I was, a kid with no legs, playing a sport where you couldn't use your hands. Still, I ran around on my hands and moved the ball along with the bottom of my torso. Mr. Gray also conceived a way for me to play golf, where I sat in my wheelchair and swung at a tennis ball with a hockey stick. Mr. Gray set up wickets around the classroom, and we aimed for those.

Mr. Gray understood how conflicted many of us in the special education wing felt. On one hand, we felt ostracized from the rest of the students at the school. At the same time, however, we never felt like we had to emulate those students. We didn't want to be treated differently, but we never wanted to feel inadequate. Mr. Gray handled this very delicately. Occasionally, he put students from both ends of the school together in the gym during recess. It made us feel like we were part of the school, and not outcasts.

Believe it or not, the one activity that brought the whole school together was dancing. Mr. Gray taught us the popular Filipino dance called Tinikling. It's a rhythmic dance, and I used the coordination I developed from it to learn how to jump rope. I started out in the middle with two people on the end twirling one rope. By elevating with my hands, I was able to jump for about 10 rotations. This was another way for me to interact with the rest of the students, and it gave me confidence that I could fit in.

Mr. Gray had this weird device that allowed people to learn to jump rope at their own pace. He took a piece of hard rubber tubing, and shaped it into a semi-circle. Then, he put spindles on each end of the tubing and attached them to four-foot-high wooden support beams. On one of the beams was a crank that he used to turn the circle, and someone would jump each time the tubing swung toward his feet—or in my case, my hands. Mr. Gray was able to turn the crank as slow as necessary, depending on who was doing the jumping. He even specialized the device for me so that I could practice jump rope without needing to have someone turn the crank. With his special device, which I wore on my back like a backpack, I was able to get about seven or eight rotations at a time. The fact that Mr. Gray was willing to do this specifically for me proved how generous and determined he was to teach each of his students. My limitations were unique from the rest of the class, yet Mr. Gray was imaginative enough to build something that made me fit in with everyone else.

Mr. Gray always joked with me that I pushed the envelope with every activity I participated in. As soon as I felt comfortable doing a certain exercise, I wanted to turn it up a notch and make it a little more difficult. My toughest challenge in Mr. Gray's class came when I was in the fourth grade. Some ropes had been hung from the ceiling in the gym, but I never paid much attention to them. On one particular day, I decided to find out about the ropes. I asked Mr. Gray what they were there for, and he challenged me to climb them. My first reaction was a unique one: I was scared. I had a fear of heights. It's a fear that's much different for someone without legs. Except for standing in my prosthesis, or sitting on a chair or couch, I never left the ground. My fear wasn't just psychological, as with someone who can't handle being in a tall building; it was also physical. If I fell even six feet through the air, I would land on my torso—be it my stomach or back—and that would hurt a lot. I don't have feet or legs to break the fall.

Without my usual confidence, I grabbed onto one of the ropes with both hands, and thought to myself, "Okay, now what?" I sat there for a couple of seconds, and then reached higher on the rope with both hands. I fell backwards. I got up, and tried it again. Same result: I fell down. Each time, I tried to pull my entire body up in one clean jerk. It happened for the duration of the class, and I was furious. It felt like the rope was taunting me, saying, "You can't get up there."

This was a new result for me—failure. I had devoted an entire class to this task, and I had made no progress. Mr. Gray had challenged me for four years by this time. I'm sure on multiple occasions, he thought he had me stumped. But even though I had struggled with some of his activities, I eventually mastered them. I thought about the first time I attempted a handstand, and remembered how difficult it was in the beginning. But after a bit of time, I figured it out.

Still, the rope looked impossible. I left class frustrated, and when I returned the next day, Mr. Gray asked my how I had fared with the rope. I told him that I couldn't do it, and I wanted to try something else. I was angry and threw a fit. He calmed me down, and explained to me that there was a certain technique to this exercise. I had to move one hand at a time, and pull myself slowly up the rope. Reluctantly, I told him I would try it the following day.

Mr. Gray was also admittedly a little nervous about the rope, because he wondered, even if I were to go up the rope, how I would get back down. Other kids who tried it were able to grip their legs around the rope and lower themselves that way. With me, I was either going to bring myself back by lowering my hands one at a time, or slide down and risk giving my hands rope burn.

The next day, when Mr. Gray wasn't looking, I went to the rope grabbed on. I moved my left hand up, and grabbed the rope a few inches higher. Then I moved my right hand above my left, but before I could grab onto the rope, I fell off. I looked around to see if anyone had seen me. Nobody came over, so I tried it again. This time, my right hand caught on to rope, and I tugged my body upward a few inches. I was making progress.

By the end of that class, I was able to move a couple feet up the rope. Within a few weeks, I got halfway to the ceiling, but that was as far as I went. I still had my fear of heights. Nevertheless, I learned a lesson that day, a pretty elementary one, but, one that would foreshadow so much of my future. I learned to never give up. Mr. Gray taught me how to do so much in my six years with him at Randall, but this was a unique lesson. He taught me that I couldn't master everything right away, and I needed to learn that.

But by the time I was eleven years old, I had accomplished just about everything Randall could offer me athletically. There were no more challenges for me there. I needed to look elsewhere.

3

Throughout my childhood, I continued to make occasional visits to Dr. Epps and Dr. Goller to make certain that my body continued to develop as it should, and make sure that my prosthesis was working properly. My mother often complained to my doctors that I liked to get out of the prosthesis and run around on my hands. My doctors reminded me how important it was to wear the legs. The more I wore them, they told me, the more comfortable I would be maneuvering in them.

Shortly after I turned five, my parents and I visited Dr. Epps for a checkup, and on the way out, his secretary stopped us. She knew how rambunctious I could get and had heard Dr. Epps implore me to wear my legs. She gave us a phone number for a wheelchair track and basketball team in Washington, D.C., named Air Capital. The team included children age six and up.

"Give them a call," she suggested to my parents. "He might like it."

My parents were familiar with such teams for children in wheelchairs but had never been approached about them. It sounded interesting to me and them. On one hand, I would be able to stay active by playing traditional sports, like basketball and track; but on the other, it also meant I had to wear my prosthesis and sit in my wheelchair. Nevertheless, my parents and I stopped by Air Capital's practice one afternoon in November 1993 in the middle of basketball season. There were about two dozens kids in wheelchairs on the court, and they all had varying physical disabilities, as well as basketball abilities.

This was the first time I had ever been on a regular basketball court. I had played at home on a mini Nerf basketball hoop, and I had also tried to dribble a regulation-size basketball. I ended up just rolling it around my apartment to get a feel for it.

"I want to try it," I told my parents.

Soon, I was partaking in basketball and track. Air Capital took its training very seriously. We practiced six days a week, only taking Sundays off. A bus picked me up from school at 2:30 in the afternoon and took me to wherever the team was practicing. We did our homework and ate dinner at practice, and the bus dropped me off at home later in the evening. I usually did not get home until 10 p.m. It was a tough schedule. I didn't get to see my parents as much as I would have liked, and all the activity was very tiring.

But it was also fun. Plus, it was convenient. The bus took me from school to practice to home, and that was important, because my parents didn't have a car at the time. I would have been bored at home because there wasn't a park or any kind of outdoor activities near our apartment, so Air Capital kept me busy and entertained.

I caught on to basketball pretty quickly. The youngest age division they had was an eight-and-under team, so I played with them. That was the one team where we didn't have to dribble. Instead, I just zipped my wheelchair around the court and snatched the ball from any unassuming opponent. I was fearless, and I charged my chair into others to get the ball. I had to learn to control myself a little bit; referees still called fouls in wheelchair basketball, and I was a little too aggressive and physical sometimes.

After that first year, I became good enough to be able to play on two teams—one with players my own age or close to it, and another with older kids. When I was eight, I played on a 12-and-under team; when I was 12, one of my teams had players who were 16, 17, and 18 years old. I later played on another team with adults, including the head coach. The coaches always tried to get me as much experience as I could stand.

We traveled a lot, which helped to broaden my horizons. In July 2000, we went to a team camp at the University of Illinois for a week, and it showed me an opportunity I never thought existed. Illinois had an entire athletic department devoted to wheelchair basketball and track. They gave out scholarships and reduced tuition costs for out-of-state students. I had watched college football and basketball on television and thought how amazing it was that those kids were able to use sports to pay for their education. I had no idea these kinds of opportunities were available to disabled athletes. This was when I first thought not only about becoming the first person in my family to go to college, but also to do so through athletics.

I liked basketball, and I might have been pretty good at it, too. One year my team finished 12th in the junior national tournament. But I really looked forward to spring and the start of track season. Speed was something that always appealed to me, probably because I had never experienced it. I couldn't ride a bike like most kids, nor could I run. I was always used to moving slower compared to everyone else. The first time I sat in a racer—a three-wheeled chair designed specifically for competition—I knew I was going to have fun with track.

It was interesting to learn how to operate a racer. The seat was more of a pocket than a chair, so I needed to install a lot of extra cushioning for my body. Then, I needed to learn how to balance the chair. Since I had no legs, there was no weight displaced to the lower part of the chair. Most people rest their legs just above that solo third wheel at the front of the racer, but in my case, my chair would tip over backwards. I had to learn to position my body in a certain way so that it wouldn't tip backward.

There is very little comparison between steering a regular wheelchair and a racer. I suppose it's tough to steer a regular wheelchair, other than accelerating it by turning the wheels. There were no axles or pivots to allow me to turn on a curve. A racer, on the other hand, needed to be able to turn when I hit the corners of the racetrack. There was a little switch near the front wheel that I had to flip in order to pivot the racer on curves. I also learned to guide the chair with my body by leaning into the turns, and leaning forward to maintain balance. It was different turning the wheels, too. In a regular chair, I move my hands from about the 12 o'clock position on the top of the wheel until I hit the four or five o'clock position. But when I needed to pick up speed in the racer, I went all the way around the clock.

I think I excelled at wheelchair sports for the same reason I had excelled at every other athletic feat I had tried in my life, because I needed to prove myself. I was usually the youngest player on my team or in my race. Since I was practicing with athletes who were four or five years older, I didn't want to come in last, or even lose. It taught me to work harder, pick up my pace, and not give an excuse if I lost, even if it was just a practice heat.

Each spring, Air Capital competed in three or four regional tournaments with the goal of qualifying for the Wheelchair Sports USA junior national meet in the summer. Each wheelchair track participant was classified according to disability. Often times, I raced against nobody. There were other athletes in my race, but they were in a different disability classification, so I wasn't actually competing against them. The regional meets were held at tracks in small towns like Fishersville, Virginia; Salisbury, Maryland; and Staunton, Virginia. The same kids were at each meet, so we knew one another and our abilities pretty well. Attendance was usually pretty sparse: the only people who watched were the athletes' parents, and sometimes they didn't make it to the meets. It was a small community, but I didn't have an alternative. This, along with the exercises and activities I did with Mr. Gray, were my only athletic outlets.

The only thing holding me back from qualifying for the national meets in 1994 was my age: I was two months too young, even though my times in the 60, 100, and 200 meters were among the fastest in the country. The following three years, I qualified easily for the junior national meets in Alabama, Washington state, and Arizona. In 1997, in Arizona, I set national records that still stand in the 100 meters (22.24 seconds), the 200 (41.70), and the 400 (1:27.44). With all of my success, my teammates called me "Big Dog," which I wrote on the side of my racer.

While I felt like I belonged with my teammates, the same wasn't necessarily true of my competition. Air Capital was comprised entirely of kids from southern and eastern Washington, D.C., and Prince George's County. We were all either African-American or Hispanic, and we stood out at meets, because the other teams were overwhelmingly white. In fact, we were called the "Black Team" after a while, and we all took a little sense of pride in that. Even though the wheelchair sports community was very open and tight-knit, our team hardly hung out with other teams. It was as much our doing as it was theirs. We felt we had nothing in common with people who were from more affluent backgrounds who didn't have to worry about the insurance pay-ments coming on time, or who could afford the little extra com-forts that insurance would not provide.

I remember one kid who raced for one of the teams in north-ern Virginia. He talked to me at a lot of the meets because he was the only black kid on his team. He never mentioned he was in an uncomfortable position, but I could tell he was. He was always so happy to see my teammates and me at meets.

Wheelchair athletes also weren't different in that we could be completely one-track minded when it came to our sport. While I was a student at Randall, Air Capital took up so much of my time that I rarely had a chance to socialize with friends, except during school hours. Air Capital eventually stopped providing a bus for us to get home each night after practice. My teammates were either 16- or 17-year-olds, or adults. Everyone except me was capable and mature enough to get home alone on the train or bus. I had just turned 12 years old, and I faced taking the train, picking up a local bus at the station, and riding that into my neighborhood at night. Then, I would have to force my wheel-chair up a steep hill for three blocks to my house. My parents were furious with the team. How could the team routinely put one of its players in such a dangerous position?

When I traveled with the adult team, I sat on the bench the majority of the time. I was there just in case someone else got hurt. If I missed a practice because of schoolwork, I was repri-manded. That bothered me, because my teammates weren't in school, and so they didn't have to worry about homework. I felt my coaches demanded a full commitment to the team, and they expected that nothing—friends, family, or even a doctor's appointment—would get in the way. I started to feel as if I was being used. If any group should understand the pain of being objectified, it should be disabled people. Yet that's exactly what they did to me.

When I began seventh grade at Kettering Middle School in the fall 2000, I began to wonder if I was missing a big part of my childhood due to athletics. It came to a point where wheelchair sports took up every moment of my spare time, and I couldn't do anything else. There were some extracurricular activities at school that interested me. I wanted to be able to hang out with my friends after school, instead of hearing stories about what they all did together the previous day while I was at practice or a meet.

After basketball season ended in early 2001, I told the team it demanded too much of my time. I never completed again with Air Capital.

Before I enrolled at Kettering, my family moved from Suitland to Fort Washington, an area in southern Prince George's County. It was a nicer apartment complex, and it was in a safer neighborhood. At Kettering, I felt like I had a chance to do things that wheelchair sports had prevented in the past. There was a television production class that met after school, and I wanted to be a part of that. I was always curious about how shows are produced. I thought it might make for an interesting career choice, so I gave it a shot. I tried several different jobs both in front of and behind the camera, and in the production room. It gave me more time to socialize and talk to people in a more relaxed atmosphere, something that I never had the opportunity to do in sports.

I also took a dance class, and that allowed me to shed my prosthesis. By that time, I had learned how to think more deeply about myself, and I had begun to develop an identity. I didn't think the prosthesis was part of that identity. I saw it as a means to deceive people. I likened them to breast implants; my legs gave people a false impression of who I was. I was proud of myself without my legs.

The most important experience I had at Kettering was being a part of the regular student body. No longer was I separated from the "normal" kids. Those two years really gave me the first shot of confidence that I could interact with everyone else. Even though Mr. Gray coordinated activities at Randall that mixed the special education classes with the rest of the student body, at the end of the day, I still went back to the special education wing. And I went back there thinking I was different.

My teachers and classmates at Kettering took a little while to warm up to me. The fact I didn't have legs didn't stun them as much as my independence did. They always tried to open the door for me, offer to push my wheelchair around, or carry my backpack. I wouldn't let them do it. My parents and Mr. Gray knew what I could do, so they never tried to help me. My first year at Kettering was the first time in my life that I had to ask people to treat me like a normal person. That surprised a lot of them, and they were a little slow to embrace it. Eventually, though, they stopped with their offers to help, and didn't think twice about whether or not I could do something on my own.

My independence caught the attention of one of my teachers, who passed my name on to a reporter at a local television station. I was the subject of a piece on the Fox affiliate's morning show. The segment discussed my extracurricular work in television production and the dance club, but it also delivered a broader message that really humbled me. The teachers and students who were interviewed for the piece all said how I was inspiration to them. My mother was right. She told me throughout my childhood that my purpose in life was to inspire people— yet nobody, besides her, had ever told me that. It humbled me to hear it.

I was 13 years old at the time, and I hadn't begun to understand some of the significant sociological issues I would encounter in the coming years. But I could tell that I was having an effect on regular people. I didn't think that what I did was unique, because it came naturally to me. Most people were genuine in the way they responded to me. Their compliments to me did not come from pity, but rather from respect and admiration.

I was also proud of how I was doing without organized sports. For three years—one at Kettering and my next two at Central High School—I didn't play any organized sports. I got home from school at three o'clock, like everyone else, and did my homework or played video games. Every so often, I threw a football around with my stepfather, Eric, or my brother, Jamar, or I went to the park with some friends, shot baskets, and did what all teenagers do best—hang out. Not having sports in my life didn't bother me. I was able to study more, and my grades made a noticeable improvement, and that was important. I had dreams of going to college, and my friends, most of whom had no ambitions beyond high school, encouraged me to aspire to that. It was almost as if they lived vicariously through my goals.

As far as I was concerned, my athletic career was over.

4

In the summer of 2002, after I graduated from Kettering Middle School, my family moved from our apartment in Fort Washington in southern Prince George's County, into our first house. It was five blocks from Southern Avenue and the Washington, D.C., city line, in a neighborhood called Capitol Heights. It was nice having our own house, even if we were just renting.

Each time we moved, my stepfather tried to get our family a little something extra, so it felt like a move up. When we moved from Suitland to Fort Washington, the new apartment complex had a pool that we could go to in the summer. The house in Capitol Heights, a neighborhood full of hilly and winding streets, was the next step up.

While having our own home was a plus, the area was hardly desirable. All sorts of litter peppered the street gutters. On every other block, there was at least one abandoned, dilapidated house, and on the property of those houses trash would be strewn across the front yard. On some blocks there were more houses with boarded windows than those with curtains. Our house was the last one on a dead-end street called Glacier Avenue. After turning onto Larchmont Avenue, you went up a steep incline before turning onto our block, which was on a decline. At the end of the block was a guardrail that separated the pavement from a large wooded area.

Since Capitol Heights was just over the border from D.C., it attracted plenty of crime; criminals would escape authorities by fleeing from one jurisdiction to the other. We would hear at least one car chase almost every night. It wasn't just police pursuing crooks; sometimes it was the result of drug deal gone bad, in which the customer was chasing the dealer, or vice versa. Several times our block played host to many of those chases. Unknowing criminals would turn onto our block, and, when they got to the end, they had a choice to make. Some barreled through the guardrail into the woods before they realized the car couldn't go far in the rugged terrain. Others abandoned their cars in front of our house, and took off on foot through the woods. Many times, we heard gunshots right outside our window.

Many of the drug deals happened at the convenience store right around the corner on Larchmont Avenue. There was a pay phone there, and in the days before cell phones, that was the command center for many transactions. Occasionally, in the day or two after an incident on or near our block, my parents would- n't let me play outside our house with my friends. They always told me that I could never tell when a car might peel around the corner, and I wouldn't have time to get out of the way.

What they didn't know was that my friends would never let that happen. I had a special group of friends when I lived in Capitol Heights. They were special not just for what they did for me, but because of when they entered my life—at a time when I was developing socially. They were a big part of that. Organized sports weren't a part of my life when I entered high school; nor were special education classes with other disabled kids. This was the first time in my life when I tried to blend in with normal people outside of school.

My next-door neighbor was Reginald Clayburn, but that was just what his birth certificate said. Everyone called him "Moo," because when he was a youngster, he used to quickly down bottles of milk. We both went to Central High School, and even though Moo was a year older than me, we hung out all the time.

It was never a problem for us to find things to do together. Moo said the door to his house was always open to me if I ever got bored or wanted to come over and watch television or play video games. But we went out a lot, too. We met up with other guys at the basketball court on Larchmont Avenue. Moo convinced the guys to let me play with them. I still had my shooting touch from when I played wheelchair basketball, but other guys wouldn't have known that if it weren't for Moo sticking up for me.

Moo sort of became my spokesperson in high school. When I was a freshman, riding through the halls in my wheelchair, other students wanted to know my story. Rather than come up to me, they went to Moo, who explained my birth, but always made sure to tell them, "Just treat him as if he was normal." That might have been the most important gesture Moo ever did for me. It was one thing for me to ask people to treat me like everyone else, but those words carried a lot more weight when they came from someone else.

Much like he did with telling people to treat me normally, Moo felt a responsibility to take care of me—as if I were his little brother, not a disabled friend. When I didn't have lunch money, Moo took care of it for me. When there was a fight or something dangerous going on, Moo made sure I got out of the way. He had a heavy guilt complex when it came to me. He wouldn't have been able to live with himself if I ever got hurt and he could have done something to prevent it. And like a big brother, Moo was a great source of advice. Early in my sophomore year, I complained to Moo that my prosthesis was hurting me. I had growth spurts that spring and summer, and the bucket was pinching me. It would be a while before I could get it fixed, and I had had enough.

"That's it," I said, as I got out of the legs and plopped down on the couch. "I'm not wearing this tomorrow."

"Yeah, that's what you've been saying for months now," Moo said. "You'll be wearing it again. I know you."

"Nah, this is it. I'm serious."

"Well, you're known around school by now," Moo responded. "If anyone says anything to you, just let me know. I'll take care of it."

And that was how I first went to school without my prosthesis. It was an invigorating feeling. I had started to develop my own personality, and the legs gave people the wrong impression of me. The first few days when I went to school without my legs, Moo walked the halls beside me, just to make sure nobody said anything out of line. He told me that was his biggest worry—someone seeing me for the first time without legs and gasping. With Moo by my side, I was confidant that things would go smoothly.

My stepfather always talked about moving out of Prince George's County, but not just because of the crime. He told me about his childhood in southern Virginia before he moved to the Washington D.C. area. With the rural countryside and the Blue Ridge Mountains as his surroundings, my stepfather could fish and hike and avoid the noise and crime of the city. I couldn't relate to that life. I was a city boy. The closest I came to fishing and hiking was spotting trash in the Potomac River and playing in the backyard of Moo's house.

As much as my stepfather thought about moving back to his rural roots, he knew he couldn't. He knew how tough it was to raise kids there, especially someone like me. There was no way I could have done wheelchair track if we had lived out in the boondocks. We would have had to travel for hours to a city where we could meet up with other wheelchair athletes. There wouldn't have been enough children like me in a rural community.

I also thought my family didn't have the money to move anywhere that could give us that quieter side of life. The Washington D.C. suburbs were too expensive, and if we moved beyond that, we would be too far away from the city's metropolitan area. We needed to be close to Prince George's County, because my stepfather's mom lived there, and my mother's family still called neighboring Charles County home.

Even if they had hit the lottery, though, I didn't want to move. I had begun my sophomore year at Central, and I finally felt like I had at Randall and Kettering—like I belonged. Other kids would refer to me as "Trevon, the guy from math class who could recite the Redskins' starting lineup." I wasn't "Trevon, the guy with no legs." In my classmates' eyes, I was one of the guys, and that was something I worked very hard to achieve.

But the decision was not up to me, and I soon learned that my parents were at least considering making another move. We had lived in our Capitol Heights house for two years when the landlord decided he wanted to sell the property. He gave my parents the first option to buy the property, so they had to make a decision: either buy the house or move again. I could see my parents' patience with Prince George's County had worn thin. One night in October, I asked my mother if we were moving. She told me that she and my stepfather were looking, but that was it.

In other words, nothing was definite. It didn't even seem like they had a plan, and that made me feel a little better about our chances of staying in our current house. My parents had often talked about big plans, like moving or buying a new car, but they never did. Something would always get in the way or pop up that caused them to forget about their plans for a while. After a few weeks, though, I noticed them coming home late from work every so often. They had files and paperwork with them that they took into their bedroom. Honestly, I was surprised—it looked like something was in the works. Were my parents actually going to follow through on one of their big plans?

One night in the middle of December, my parents came home and hit me with the news: "We're moving! We're moving!" my mother screamed as she walked through the door with her arms raised. "We signed the papers! We're moving!" I looked over at my stepfather to see if maybe this was my mother's idea of a joke. He just smiled and nodded. I dropped my chin into my chest and gathered my thoughts. The reaction I showed next would either make my parents even happier or crush them. I knew how much they wanted this, and their faces showed it. I couldn't remember if I had ever seen them this happy. So I picked my head up, looked at them with a smile, and said, "That's great."

But I wasn't celebrating. I was worried about leaving my high school and my friends. Regardless of where we moved, I wanted to stay at Central because of how comfortable I felt with my class-mates. I didn't even want to know where we were moving. I knew it was going to be far from Capitol Heights, and that meant I would have to leave this life behind.

As my parents took off their coats, I went into my bedroom, lay down on my bed, and started to cry. I had done enough acting for one night. I was furious with them. I didn't feel like I had any say in the decision or that they had been up front with me about the chance of us moving. They never asked me, "Hey, Trey, if we were to move, how would you feel about it?" I didn't have an opportunity to plead my case or change their minds. It was too late.

I had three months to prepare myself before the moving truck arrived to take us to our new home. Nothing worked. I was in denial. Gradually, my parents packed boxes with our belongings. I still didn't know where we were moving, and my parents never told me. They were smart. They knew that if they did tell me, it would only start a fight.

A week before the move, I told my stepfather flatly, "I'm not going. I'm staying here." I figured I could live with Moo. "This is my house and my rules," my stepfather told me. "You're going." I realized I had no choice when I came home from school on a Friday afternoon in March, and there was a U-haul truck parked outside of our house. My Uncle Charles and my grandmother were there to help my parents load up the truck and their cars. I gave everyone the silent treatment. All the while, though, I worried that if family members were there to help, then we must be headed far away.

The sun had set by the time we hit the road. I rode with my grandmother. We followed my uncle, who drove the U-Haul, and behind us were my mother in her car and my stepfather in his. We drove through the streets of Capitol Heights and turned left onto Route 4, heading out of town. As we traveled along, the strip malls and traffic lights gave way to trees and darkness. I thought about falling asleep, especially if we were moving hundreds of miles away.

After about 45 minutes on Route 4, the scenery became a mix of strip malls interspersed with open farm fields. Finally, we turned off the road, and I saw a community unlike any in Capitol Heights. I could hardly make out what we were passing because there were no streetlights. But for every house I saw, there was a huge open field separating it from the next house. In Capitol Heights, houses were right next to one another. It didn't seem like people lived close to one another in this place.

I'll never forget the first time I saw the sign for "Deep Landing Road." Oh no, I thought. Not only were we moving to a place in the middle of nowhere, but also there was a street that described it perfectly. We drove down a short hill and then were greeted on both sides of a two-lane road by enormous farm fields.

"You see that?" my grandmother pointed far ahead.

"Uh, no," I said.

"That's your new house."

My heart sank. I couldn't see anything, but I didn't need to. I knew there wasn't anything to see. All four cars pulled into the driveway. As I opened the car door, the first thing I noticed wasn't the house, but the huge field adjacent to it. My parents, grandmother, and uncle all gushed about how peaceful and quiet the area was. To myself, I complained for the same reasons they rejoiced. What could a 15-year-old do for fun around here? Who could he have fun with?

"Where are we?" I asked.

"This is Huntingtown, Maryland," my stepfather said. "Calvert County. It's beautiful."

I had never heard of Calvert County, but it was just south of Prince George's County in Maryland. I immediately thought, "How am I going to get to Central?" I was going to have to wake up at 4 a.m. just to make it to school on time.

We unpacked the U-Haul and loaded our beds into the house and went to sleep. I didn't really care to look around at our new house. I just wanted to go to sleep and hopefully wake up in Capitol Heights the following morning and realize this was a bad dream. Of course, when I woke up the next day, I went outside and looked at that field on the other side of our driveway, and knew this was no dream. This really was the middle of nowhere, and it scared me. It didn't look like anywhere I had ever visited, let alone lived.

Our house was at one end of a long, straight road that eventually bent around a corner and disappeared into more open fields. I could see almost a mile into the distance from my driveway, because there were no trees on our side of the road, just open fields of corn and beans that belonged to our neighbor who lived a half-mile away. There were houses across the street from ours that didn't have farms but still had plenty of land. In fact, all of the properties in the neighborhood, whether or not they housed farms, were spread out. I couldn't talk to a neighbor from my front yard like I could at my old house in Capitol Heights. This didn't feel like a community, and that bothered me. What I loved the most about Capitol Heights was knowing there was always someone close by, whether he was next door, across the street, or even a couple of houses down. I never had to go far for company.

We drove back out to Route 4 to eat breakfast at a restaurant in one of the strip malls. These weren't malls, though, where I could see myself hanging out. Each one usually had a big store, like a supermarket or a K-Mart, and then about a half-dozen or so small stores flanking it like a Subway, a nail salon, or an auto parts store. When I lived in Capitol Heights, the Forestville mall was a five-minute drive from our house. Not only was that mall indoors, but it had a department store, good clothing stores, a couple music stores, and places to eat. It was somewhere we could hang out. I soon found out that the closest mall to my new house in Huntingtown was almost an hour away, and I had to rely on my parents to drive me there.

As we drove, I noticed there were plenty more farms blanketing the landscape before we reached the main road. I didn't see any parks or playgrounds, like the one on Larchmont Avenue in Capitol Heights that I went to on a regular basis. I wondered where kids went to hang out, or how they even made friends. It seemed like people were trapped in their houses. There were also little subdivisions of huge houses that seemed just recently built. These had to be the ones that attracted the new families who moved into

Calvert County. By the time I moved there, Calvert was the fastest-growing county in Maryland, primarily because families loved the affordable housing, safe community, and good schools.

Many of the people we saw, though, didn't look like us. I looked at the people in the cars we passed along the way, and nearly everyone was white. It was more of the same at the restaurant where we ate breakfast. I didn't dislike white people. I just wondered how these people would treat a black family, obviously a very small minority in the community.

As we drove back home, I asked my stepfather what I would do about school. He told me I could go to Central High School for the rest of the school year, but I would go to a school in Calvert County at the start of my junior year. Since he worked as a parts salesman at a car dealership not too far from Central, he would drive me to school each morning.

"I want to graduate with my friends at Central," I told him. "Can I stay with Moo?"

"No, you're going to school here," he responded. "Don't worry. You'll make new friends."

But I wasn't ready to say goodbye to my old ones. When I went to school on Monday, I told my friends about the move. They couldn't believe my parents had actually done it, either.

"Oh, now you're gonna start talking like a redneck," Moo said. "Like, 'Howdy, boy.'"

I sat in class the rest of the day and thought about what Moo said. My new school was going to be a completely different environment than Central. Each time I had started at a new school in my life, I was always looked at as being different. I was used to being singled out because of the way I looked. It took time to become accepted, and I had spent a year and a half working to become a part of the school community at Central. All of a sudden, I had to leave. And where was I headed? To a new school, where I would be singled out because I was black. Race was never an issue I had to face at my other schools. Never mind that I would have to start all over and explain why I didn't have any legs. I was really angry with my parents; even though they told me they made the move in order to ensure my safety, I didn't want to listen to their reasoning.

On my last day of school in June, my mother drove me to Central. Not long after we pulled out onto Route 4 and headed north, she pointed to a construction site on our right.

"That's where you'll be going to school next year," she told me.

Calvert County's rapid growth had forced its three existing public high schools—Calvert, Northern, and Patuxent—to become overcrowded. So a fourth was being built: Huntingtown High School was scheduled to open that fall. Most of the high schools I had seen before looked nothing like this building, which was still under construction. Huntingtown High School sat along Route 4, between two wooded areas, and had a huge parking lot in front of it. The site used to be a farm. I couldn't see any sports fields or campus where students would hang out, but that was because the building stretched wide across the lot and extended far back into it. It looked more like an office building than a school. It was three stories high and had a very modern design.

Central, on the other hand, sat at the end of a narrow tree-lined and wooded street. It was a small building; the second floor, in fact, only had a few classrooms. Just from the look of the building, I knew that going to Huntingtown would be a shock to my system.

Once my mother and I arrived at Central, I went to class to pick up my final report card, and she went into the main office to disenroll me from the school. Nothing about the move—not the initial drive to the strange place, not waking up to the sight of a farm, not driving an hour to and from school every day—affected me quite like this final trip to Central. My life at Central was over, and I knew, at last, that it was for real.

Summer was usually the highlight of the year for me. In years past, I had taken so many exciting trips with Air Capital. Time flew so fast; I was usually not ready for school to resume in September. But the summer after my sophomore year at Central was far and away the worst for me. Time seemed to stand still. I was confused. Part of me didn't want the summer to end because it meant that I would have to start school at Huntingtown. But the other part of me couldn't bear one more moment of the summer. I was bored senseless at my new home in the country.

Three days after school ended, I realized that I was stuck in the middle of nowhere. I didn't know anybody in the neighborhood or even in the county for that matter. On the way to the supermarket one afternoon, I saw what the teenagers in Calvert County did for fun: They drove their cars to the parking lots of strip malls along Route 4, parked, blasted their stereos, and just hung out. It seemed pathetic. And that wasn't because I couldn't drive. How could just hanging out in a parking lot possibly be any fun?

I spent a lot of time that summer with Moo and my friends in Capitol Heights. My stepfather told me he didn't want me hanging out up there because of how dangerous it was, but he knew how upset and lonely I was in Huntingtown. Without school, I was trapped in my house, unable to meet new friends. My parents weren't about to cut my only friends out of my life, so they allowed me to stay at Moo's house for several days at a time.

Moo always asked me about Huntingtown. He was very curious about a place he had never visited. I told him about the farms and about the kids driving to the parking lots. Other than that, I didn't want to talk about it, because it depressed me. It was one thing for people to hear about it and say how sorry they felt for me, but it was worse to have to experience it. Moo and my friends knew that; they never came down to visit me because it was too far a drive for them.

My stays at Moo's house grew shorter as the summer wore on. Before I knew it, it was early August, and it was time to enroll at my new school. It was two weeks before the first day of school, and construction was still not finished at Huntingtown. They were hurrying to finish it up, and it gave me another ray of hope: What if the first day of school came and the building wasn't ready yet? Maybe I could go back to Central. But that was not the case: the construction was completed and Huntingtown was ready to open for Day One of my junior year of high school.

For my first day at a new school, my mother suggested an old friend join me—my prosthesis. As much as I hated wearing them, I knew the legs helped me fit in a little better, and my mother wanted me to feel comfortable. But when we went to get the prosthesis out of the closet, we could see that the bucket was now too small for me. My mother and I looked at the device and she agreed there was no way I could wear it.

It worried me, though, because I had to go to a new school and meet people without my legs. I knew I would already stick out because I was black and I used a wheelchair. Once the rest of the students saw that I didn't have legs, I was worried about becoming a spectacle.

Jamar and I talked the night before about how we thought people would receive us at the school. We had no idea what to expect. How many other black kids would there be at the school? Would they pick on us because we were the new kids? I told Jamar, "You've gotta watch my back, and I'll watch yours."

Jamar and I took separate buses to school, since I had to ride on a bus suited for my wheelchair. As soon as I got to school, I was overwhelmed at how big the place was. I had heard of schools with much larger student bodies than the 1,500 at Huntingtown, but the building was so spread out. I had been to the school one night the previous week for a student orientation, but we all met in the auditorium. They didn't let us walk around the school, because construction was still going on. I went to my first day of classes with the map I received at the orientation, yet I was still confused. Luckily, I was able to find the elevator easily, and that allowed me to get upstairs with my wheelchair. I sat quietly in each of my classes, and I didn't notice any strange looks. Of course, a few people pointed in my direction. But the looks on their faces indicated they wondered what was up with the new guy, instead of what was up with the new guy *with no legs.*

I ate lunch during fourth period, the earliest lunch of the day at 10:10 a.m. I looked around the cafeteria and saw the cliques of students sitting at separate tables. Even though Huntingtown was a new school, its student body was drawn from the county's three other high schools; everyone there had a group of friends from their old high school, and besides, as I learned, Calvert County is a very close community. There were a number of black students at the school, but they were still a small minority. The change was a shock to my system, considering that Capitol Heights is nearly 93 percent black. I could probably count the number of white students at Central on one hand.

I found an empty table and rolled my wheelchair up to it. I sat alone at lunch for the first time in years. The cliques were established at Huntingtown. The kids from Northern hung out in one section. Calvert kids were in another group. Patuxent kids were in a third corner. Everyone knew someone else, except me. Nobody wanted to sit with the black kid in the wheelchair.

Lunch lasted only 30 minutes but it felt a lot longer. It only took a few seconds for me to whisper to myself, "I hate it here." I don't know how many times I repeated that phrase in my head during that half hour. Nobody talked to me during my afternoon classes, and I didn't talk to anyone. At dismissal, I took the same bus home and climbed into bed for a nap. Every bad idea I had about leaving Central, I thought, was proven true that first day at Huntingtown. I was an outcast. I had nothing in common with these kids. Capitol Heights might have been less than an hour from my new home, but it was practically another world away, as far as I was concerned. The kids at Huntingtown lived in subdivisions with manicured lawns or on sprawling farmland with front yards big enough for a small football field. They spent their summers at the beach and their winters on the ski slopes. We shared nothing in common. They wanted nothing to do with me, and I didn't want anything to do with them.

My parents asked me about my day, and I told them it was pretty quiet and uneventful. My stepfather asked me how many black kids there were in my classes.

"None in my first period," I said. "None in the second. One in the third. None in the fourth. Umm, none the rest of the day."

"Okay," my mother said. "You're going to have to make some friends."

The next day was nearly the exact same routine. But it started to change at the beginning of my fifth-period biology class. My teacher was Kristin Hunter, who was 22 years old and just one year out of college. She was different from most teachers, in that she was young enough to relate to high school students. Ms. Hunter started to talk to me before class began. She knew I had just moved from Capitol Heights, and what a huge change of culture that was for me.

"Are you feeling comfortable here?" she asked. "Are you fitting in?"

"Um, I guess." I said.

"What do you mean? Are people weird to you?"

"Yeah, they are. They're kind of scared to come up to me."

At least they had been up until my third day of school. On Day Three, I sat silent through my morning classes, and then I went to my same lonely table in the cafeteria for lunch. I was in for a surprise.

"Do you wanna join us?" asked a soft voice on my left.

I looked up and saw these two girls—two white girls. They introduced themselves as Jessie Moulton and Alyssa Finlayson.

"We're going to get lunch," Jessie said. "Can we leave our books here and join you when we get back?"

I nodded, but I was shocked. I wasn't expecting anyone to come up to me, especially so early in the school year. I figured it would take a couple of weeks before I met people like this. I had met students when I started at Kettering or Central through interaction in class. I could always count on a situation that forced dialogue with someone to break the ice. At Huntingtown, I thought I would have to go over to other kids and start a conversation. Jessie and Alyssa, though, came up to me. Ms. Hunter was an assistant coach for Huntingtown's girls' soccer team. Jessie was the team's captain, and Alyssa also played for them. Ms. Hunter knew how outgoing Jessie was and encouraged her to find me in the cafeteria and talk to me.

We discussed our classes; Jessie was a sophmore and Alyssa a junior. We got bored of that pretty quickly, though, so Jessie figured it was time to ask the important questions.

"So, how'd you get into that wheelchair? Were you born like that?" she asked.

I hadn't rehearsed what to say to anyone who asked me about my condition, because I didn't expect to have to talk to anyone. This caught me a little off-guard, but I was grateful to Jessie and Alyssa for offering to talk. The least I could do was be honest.

"I was born without legs," I said.

"Really?" Jessie asked.

"Yeah, it's a common thing," I told her, and then explained what congenital amputation is and how often it occurs.

"Wow, there were rumors going around school," she said, "that you were in a car accident or something like that."

I shook my head and smiled. "People love to make stuff up about me. They just really don't know. That bothers me."

"I'm sorry," Jesse said. "But thanks for telling us about it."

"I'm glad you asked. When people just assume things, that's how rumors get started."

And that was it. We didn't talk anymore about my condition. Jessie and Alyssa, instead, asked me about Capitol Heights. I began to realize that they had no idea how different our lives were, and I was happy to tell them about it. Then Jessie told me about my new classmates, pointing out different people scattered throughout the cafeteria. We talked about all the cliques, and soon I had identities to place with these new faces. These people suddenly intrigued me.

Before I knew it, lunchtime was over and we had to go back to class. We had a wonderful conversation, and it was just what I needed. I had never spoken to white girls before, but that didn't matter. I was desperate for friends, and I realized I was lucky to have met these girls. I was so grateful to Ms. Hunter for asking Jessie and Alyssa to talk to me that I brought her a package of cookies from lunch every day for about a month as a sign of my appreciation.

That half-hour with Jessie and Alyssa let me know that there was a place for me at Huntingtown. Maybe it would be with them, or with other cliques. But it was clear that there would be chances for me to find my comfort zone. Opportunities sometimes come from the most unexpected places.

5

By my second week at my new high school, my attitude had changed dramatically. It became a lot easier to get on the bus each morning because I knew there were people to talk to at the end of the ride. That first conversation with Jessie and Alyssa didn't just open doors for me to other people at the school, it also eased so many of the fears and sources of tension I had about leaving Central High School and coming to Huntingtown. I saw, through Jessie and Alyssa, that my new classmates could accept me and be friendly with me. It appeared to me that I had nothing in common with these girls, yet they did not let that stand in the way of starting a friendship.

Over the next two weeks, I listened to Jessie and Alyssa talk about what it was like growing up in the suburbs and what their interests were. Their lives differed from my life in Prince George's County. It was interesting, but very difficult to relate my life to theirs. Nobody could go anywhere in Calvert County without a car. People did not use public transportation. There wasn't a bus that I could pick up around the corner from my house and take it to the Metro train station 10 minutes away. People didn't live in communities where they could walk out of their homes and go to the corner store for a soda.

At the same time, they didn't know what it was like to have violence as an everyday fact of life. Guns weren't a factor, except for the rifles their relatives kept to go hunting. They didn't know people who got arrested, mugged, or shot. Police officers, more often than not, were friendly to residents in the suburbs. In Capitol Heights, they were seen as enemies.

It was hard to do anything out of the ordinary in Calvert County without everybody hearing about it. The environment was very similar to what my mother endured growing up in La Plata, Maryland, just on the other side of the Patuxent River. In communities like Huntingtown, people grew to know one another very well because all the activities were limited to the local residents. The community had its own activities planned for its members. Outsiders didn't exist, and the insiders hardly ever left. When someone did, it was news. Families moved to Calvert County to get away from the elements that made inner-city communities so undesirable. It was such a contrast from Prince George's County, where I remember seeing kids in school one day and then never again. Nobody knew what happened to them, and when I told people at Huntingtown about this, the part that stunned them the most was that, after a few days, nobody cared what happened to those people.

Jessie told me she was going to play for Huntingtown's varsity girls' basketball team that winter. She introduced me to a few of the players and suggested I be the team manager. There were plenty of jobs for me to do—help the coaching staff organize each practice, run the scoreboard and clock during drills, and keep statistics and update the scorebook during games. It sounded like so much fun. This was my first chance to be a part of a team that was open to everyone, not just people with disabilities. As much as I told people that I didn't miss participating in wheelchair sports, the previous four years had been tough on me. I had a very competitive streak inside me, and no matter how many times I beat Moo in video games, it just didn't satisfy me quite like being in the action.

I was excited about getting back into sports, and I knew my parents would be proud of me. Later that night, my stepfather and I were watching television and I told him about it. I couldn't wait for him to tell me how happy he was that I was trying to fit into the community. I kind of expected him to tell me "I told you so," and remind me of how pessimistic I was about finding anything to do at the school. But I was wrong. My stepfather was disappointed in me.

"Why are you going to sit around and watch people play?" he asked. I explained to him that being a team manager would accomplish two goals for me—be involved with sports and meet new people who would help me make more friends at the school.

"Don't you want to play?" he asked.

"Yeah, but I can't. There are no wheelchair sports," I responded.

"What about wrestling?"

I rocked backward and laughed hysterically.

I didn't know what was sillier about wrestling: the singlet, which was the tight outfit the wrestlers wore, or how they clutched, grabbed, and put their hands all over their opponent's body. I knew one thing for sure about wrestling: it looked uncomfortable and homosexual, and I didn't want to touch a guy like that. I wanted nothing to do with wrestling.

My stepfather didn't laugh along with me, though. When I told him I thought wrestling was ridiculous, he surprised me with his response.

"You know, I wrestled in high school," he said.

"You used to wrestle?' I replied with shock. "I thought it was for skinny people."

I looked at my stepfather, who had gained a fair amount of weight since he wrestled at 185 pounds for Forestville High in 1986. Then I remembered him watching wrestling on television when it came on during the Summer Olympics. He had tried to teach me about the sport, how wrestlers have to be so aware of every part of their bodies during a match, and how even the slightest move could determine the outcome of an Olympic match. While I pretended to pay attention, I could not understand his fascination with the sport and its strategy. It was just too funny to look at these guys in tights grabbing each other.

"No, stop laughing," he told me. "With your strength, you could be good."

"Stop playing," I said. "I don't want to do that."

"It's just like chess," he explained. "You play your opponent, and you plan your moves. It's a sport that's all in your mind."

He was starting to get me worried. Was he serious about this? It was one thing for me to be a manager on a team with normal players, but I couldn't compete against them. There were too many reasons why I couldn't wrestle. For starters, what did I know about wrestling? All I knew was what I saw on the WWE, like jumping off the corners to body-slam guys, or hitting them with chairs. And that couldn't be further from an Olympic sport.

My stepfather laughed, just like I did at his initial suggestion. "It's nothing like that," he said. "Okay," I thought to myself. "If he didn't buy that argument, what about this one?"

"What about my desire to be part of a team?" I asked him. "I love playing wheelchair basketball, but in wheelchair track, I'm always out there by myself. With wrestling, there's only two people on the mat—one against one. Where's the team?"

"That's what's so great about wrestling," he answered. "It's a team sport because you and the rest of your teammates each have to wrestle and earn points to beat the other team. But it's also an individual sport, and I know how much you love being able to control the outcome. Even if Air Capital didn't win the team title at a track meet, you were still first in your races."

He was right about that, too. I had only one argument left.

"Um, hello? Did you forget something? How am I going to move around and beat guys who have legs?" I asked him.

"Look at yourself," he said, smiling. "Your arms are as long as their bodies. You're low to the ground, so you can shoot in at their legs. You can learn some moves, and you'll be good. With your strength and weight, you could dominate."

I was still skeptical, but with the confidence he seemed to have in me, my interest increased. He explained to me how wrestling could afford me the contact I craved in sports, but couldn't get from any wheelchair events. I had always wanted to play football, but that just didn't seem possible. At least with wrestling, I could hit people.

"But I've got to warn you," he added. "It's tough. You've got to be in the best condition of your life. You're going to have to do a lot of running."

Whoa, I thought. Forget about putting on the tight singlet. Forget about grabbing another guy around his thighs. I could teach myself to handle that. But how in the heck was I going to run? How does someone without legs run?

"What do you mean by a lot of running?" I asked.

"It all depends on your coach, but my coach used to have us run laps on the track, a few miles. It was all part of our conditioning. We had to be ready to be at full strength for six minutes. That's how long a wrestling match lasts—three periods, two minutes each period.

"It's a good way to keep in shape," he laughed.

There was a hidden message in that laugh. He was reminiscing about his high school days, and that brought back fond memories. But that chuckle also taunted me a bit. It wasn't to insult me, but rather, to motivate me. My stepfather knew how much I loved challenges and proving people wrong. I viewed my whole life as a challenge, and every endeavor was a chance to prove myself. This, however, was going to be my biggest challenge, if I decided to do it. I thought about the awkwardness, my lack of knowledge of the sport, and my inherent disadvantage of competing against people with two legs. Could there possibly be a bigger challenge?

"Okay, I'll give it a shot," I told him.

"Well, then," he said, "you go to school tomorrow, find the wrestling coach, shake his hand, and tell him, 'Hi, I'm your 103-pounder.'"

I abandoned my plans of becoming a basketball manager and decided to try my stepfather's wild idea. As I fell asleep that night, I wondered if I had just made a promise I would soon regret.

When I went to Huntingtown for orientation before the school year had begun, the first person I met was one of the vice principals. "If you ever need anything around here," vice principal Dave Taylor told me, "you come talk to me."

Mr. Taylor had worked in Calvert County for more than two decades, and was a vice principal at Calvert High before taking the same job at Huntingtown when it opened. He was very interested in sports at the school, and he was always at games, both at the school, and elsewhere within the county. It was time for me to take Mr. Taylor up on his offer to help. I needed to ask him to introduce me to the school's wrestling coach. I had no idea who that was. I spotted Mr. Taylor in the hallway that day, and he smiled when I came up to him.

"Hey, Mr. Taylor, I need to ask you a question," I said. "My dad told me to come talk to you about trying out for the wrestling team. I don't know who the coach is."

Any other teacher might have thought I was nuts. I probably would have received one of those playful smiles, followed by, "Oh, that's so amazing that you want to try wrestling, but I don't think it's right for you."

But Mr. Taylor's response was different. My request didn't stun him or make him uneasy. In fact, he was happy to hear it. "Don't worry, Trevon. I'll talk to the wrestling coach, and see what you need to do."

Unbeknownst to me, before he went into school administration, Mr. Taylor had coached wrestling for more than a decade, first at Potomac High in Prince George's County, and then at Calvert High, just a few miles down Route 4 from where Huntingtown opened. Like my stepfather, he knew wrestling could accommodate someone like me. He had heard about people with similar conditions who tried the sport.

The following morning, a Friday, there was a knock on the door while I was in Mr. Johnson's math class. Mr. Taylor was outside and wanted to see me.

"Trevon," he said, with a proud grin, "This is Coach Green, our wrestling coach."

Terry Green looked like the typical former wrestler. He was short and stocky and looked as if he could snarl with the meanest guys in a room. He looked tough, like someone I would want on my side of a fight. That came from a lifetime of being involved in wrestling. He grew up in Jamestown, New York, just off Lake Erie, near the state's southwestern border with Pennsylvania. He started wrestling when he was eight years old, primarily because that was his only choice. The local youth baseball and football leagues required participants to be nine, but the wrestling league took eight-year-olds.

He grew to love the sport. After a record of 101-19 at Jamestown High School, including a fifth-place finish in the state his senior year, Coach Green went on to wrestle at Edinboro College in northwestern Pennsylvania. He graduated from there in 1993 and then took a teaching job at Lackey High School in Southern Maryland, where he also was named an assistant wrestling coach. After three years as an assistant, he took over the Lackey program before the 1996-97 season and led it to the 1997 state championship.

As I would soon learn, Coach Green was soft-spoken, smart, and chose his words carefully. Above all else, he was patient, and that was a critical asset for his new job—teaching special education at Huntingtown.

"It would be an honor to have you come to our open mat," Coach Green said, with a warm, confident smile as he shook my hand. "We'll teach you the basics, and you'll do fine."

Even though tryouts didn't start for another two months, Coach Green opened the wrestling room every Monday and Wednesday evenings for kids to get a little practice. It was called "open mats" and it was wrestling's version of playing pickup basketball games. Sometimes there were a dozen guys there, and other times there were just a couple. Guys wrestled whoever was there, which meant that two wrestlers of differing weights would often wrestle each other. It forced everyone to use the time to work on technique, and experiment with new moves. For me, it would be a chance to learn moves. Any moves.

I headed back into class after my meeting with Coach Green with a big smile; his offer had left me beaming. For the first time that I could remember, I wished it wasn't a Friday. I didn't want to have to wait a whole weekend until I could get to the next open mat. Suddenly, I was excited to try wrestling and all that it included—the competition, the team camaraderie, and the chance to learn something completely new.

I thought about Coach Green and how tough he looked. When he spoke, I saw a warm and caring side to him that came across in his handshake and the tone of his voice. I considered that to be a good insurance policy for when it came time to start wrestling. Even though Jessie and Alyssa had proven to be so welcoming and friendly, I wasn't ready to completely let my guard down and assume everyone in the Huntingtown student body would be just as kind.

I was no fool. This was high school. Teenage boys are moody, completely unpredictable, and some of them love to be obnoxious when they are among a group of friends. I had seen it happen when seniors picked on freshmen, or football players taunted the kids who weren't jocks. The strong kids take advantage of the weak. It's always been that way in high school, and there was no doubt to which group I belonged. I envisioned the possibility of going to the open mat on Monday, and entering a room full of cocky guys laughing when they saw me. "Who is this freak?" they would ask each other. I imagined them making jokes, calling me names, and avoiding me because, well, nobody wanted to be near the black kid with no legs.

But those thoughts didn't intimidate me. Instead, they motivated me to prove that I belonged. Monday couldn't get here quick enough.

6

Algebra was the furthest thing from my mind.

"Trevon Jenifer? Trevon!"

"Oh, here, Mr. Johnson."

I daydreamed so much in each of my classes the following Monday that I didn't even pay attention to roll call. All I thought about was the open mat later that evening. I spent the weekend imagining my first day as a wrestler and my debut competing against normal people. It had been three full days since I met Coach Green outside of my math class, but I had thought of little since then but my debut on the mat.

School dismissed at 2:30, but open mat didn't start until six o'clock. I had to find a way to kill the time. It was still early in the school year, and homework didn't take that long. I decided to zip my wheelchair around the lobby outside of the entrance to the gymnasium. This lobby was where anyone who played on a team hung out while waiting for practice to start. It was a very social scene. Since school was out and the teachers had all gone home, there wasn't the threat of discipline looming. I struck up a conversation with some of the people who passed by or were waiting for others.

It was there that I learned my wheelchair could be the perfect icebreaker for conversations with girls. I pulled up beside a group of girls, and asked if one of them would like a ride. We sped down the hallway laughing, and before I knew it, girls were fighting for the next spot in my chair.

Shortly before 6, my stepfather walked into the school. He came straight from work, because I think he was even more excited than I was about the open mat. Over the weekend, he used every moment we were together to talk to me about wrestling. He stood in our living room, and mimicked some moves I should try on the mat. With each move, he pointed out the muscles critical to executing it, and told me how important it was for me to strengthen those muscles. Each of his stories found its way to a tangent that led into a memory from his wrestling career. On and on he went. It was hard for me to stay interested, because I still didn't understand anything about this sport, but I tried. I saw how much my decision to wrestle meant to him.

As much as my stepfather supported and encouraged me athletically throughout my childhood, there was always a disconnection, and it was pretty easy to see why that happened: We could never share experiences with each other. When I was in my wheelchair speeding around the track, he couldn't ride in the lane beside me. He couldn't relate to what I did. He hadn't spent a moment of his life in a wheelchair.

There is something very All-American about a father and son playing catch or a game of one-on-one in the driveway. Each family has its watershed moment when the father realizes his son's fastball has such velocity that it hurts his hand when it lands in his glove. It's a part of growing up, and at that moment, the father realizes how quickly time has passed him by. And here it was, when my stepfather and I walked into the wrestling room together, that he finally had his chance to share a sports moment with his son.

I was so nervous about how that moment would begin. I dismounted from my wheelchair, strutted into the room, and found it nearly empty. Only four other kids were there. That was already a small victory for me. I wasn't on display for the entire program, and without a dozen or so friends to hide behind, none of those guys were going to say anything that could offend me. I went straight for the right corner of the room and changed into a pair of shorts and a T-shirt. I was ready to learn.

My first lesson was surprising one. As I stretched my arms and back, I occasionally peered over to the other kids in the room. A couple of times, I caught them staring at me, but I could tell it was genuine curiosity and nothing mean-spirited. They almost forgot we were there to wrestle. Instead, they just wanted to see me move around on my hands.

Coach Green came over and introduced himself to my stepfather. There was one other kid in the room who was close enough to me in weight, and he wound up wrestling on Huntingtown's junior varsity team that season. Coach Green put us together on a mat, and my wrestling career officially began. I could tell my opponent was a little hesitant to make contact with me, especially any part of my body below my chest. I was used to this. Every time I did some sort of physical activity with two-legged people, they were always worried they would hurt me. For some reason, I looked fragile in their eyes. I don't know why. Nothing on me was broken; it was just missing.

Anyway, we rolled around on the mat for about an hour. My stepfather kept yelling, "Shoot. Shoot," and I didn't know what he was talking about. Apparently, that was the term for making a move at an opponent's legs. I later found out that it's a pretty common term. Obviously, I had a lot to learn. I didn't talk much during that hour. I just listened to my stepfather shout instructions. I was confused, but that didn't slow me down. In hindsight, I probably didn't execute any of the moves correctly, but I kept on trying. Coach Green closed up the room after about an hour, which was fine with me. I was exhausted.

On the drive home, I thought about how much work I had ahead of me. There was no way I could give this anything less than a full effort. If I wasn't totally committed to learning everything I could about the sport—and that meant absorbing every one of my stepfather's sermons—then I shouldn't continue. I knew I could do this, but there was still a lingering feeling of awkwardness that I had to overcome. I convinced myself that I would become more comfortable with more time on the mat.

"That was fun, wasn't it?" my stepfather asked.

"Yeah, it's okay," I stammered. "I liked it."

Deep down, I wondered how good I could be. Even with 100 percent dedication to the sport, I was not sure that I could reach the level that would satisfy me. The last time I competed in an organized sport—wheelchair track—I set national records that still stood. That was my standard. It was a tall one, but still, one that I had to uphold. I didn't handle failure well.

Two days later, I came back to Wednesday's open mat. Nobody was particularly surprised to see me this time around. I knew they watched me while I wrestled on Monday. They saw that I was active and listening to suggestions. They didn't hear me complaining or see me get frustrated. I hadn't convinced them yet, though, that I was there to stay. Maybe that was because I hadn't convinced myself of that yet.

I spent the next two months trying to sway myself. I came to every open mat on Mondays and Wednesdays until practice officially started on November 15. I spent a lot of time studying other wrestlers. I tried to copy their moves, but this was like running before I learned how to walk. They had been working on their moves for a couple of years, sometimes longer than that. Their moves were all derived from the fundamental maneuvers, which I hadn't yet learned.

My saving grace, early on, was my ability to score takedowns relatively easily. I was low to the ground and had a clear shot at my opponent's knees. Plus, when guys wrestled me, they had to lean over to get close enough to me, and that put them a little bit off-balance, which I tried to use to my advantage. Takedowns, for me, were a product of strength, and that was all I had then. I had neither skill nor technique yet.

As important as it was for me to grow comfortable on the mat, it was even more crucial to erase any remaining uneasiness with the other wrestlers. In order for these guys to be my team-mates, we all had to develop a level of trust with one another. If there was one lesson shared over those two months prior to the start of practice, it was that they did not have to be so care-ful with me. Once they started plowing into me, and using their full strength against me, I felt like I had achieved something with them.

Also during those two months, Coach Green did a lot of homework. He read about other wrestlers who were missing limbs. He tried to learn what techniques they employed that made them successful wrestlers, and studied how the human body worked. There was a story that gained national attention a year earlier about a high-schooler in Georgia named Kyle Maynard, who was also a congenital amputee. He was born with no elbows or knees. Maynard finished his senior season 35-16, and reached the Georgia state tournament.

Coach Green had seen plenty of unique cases in person. He told me about one from when he was in high school. His team faced a wrestler who had no legs below the knees and no fingers. Coach Green said that the kid's courage to get out on the mat amazed him more than any victory the kid had. That was Coach Green's subtle way of inspiring and motivating me.

When practice started, I was one of 26 kids who jammed into the wrestling room. Most of the other wrestlers were unfamiliar to me, as many of them hadn't been coming to open mats. They all had one thing in common—they were white. I never had to reconcile race before, largely because I was rarely in a diverse environment. Every school I had attended—Randall, Kettering, and Central—was overwhelmingly black. Air Capital was the same. I never had to play with white kids, just against them.

It was as if I took one step forward when Jessie and Alyssa befriended me in the cafeteria, and then I took two steps backward when I entered this wrestling room. Lunch was a half-hour each day, and I could move from one table if I wasn't comfortable. Practice lasted three hours, and I was trapped in a cramped room with no windows. I needed to fit in all over again.

I could tell the majority of the other wrestlers were eyeing me. Part of their curiosity was whether I was some sort of superstar, as if I had some hidden strength—like incredibly powerful arms—that allowed me to overcome my lack of legs. That had to be the case, they thought, because from the looks of me, my presence had to be some kind of joke. I noticed a lot of double-takes and guys leaning over to whisper to their friends, "Hey, check him out." It made me a little nervous. I worried that they were going to watch every move I made, and if I messed up, pounce on me with criticism.

Just before Coach Green started talking, one of the seniors came up to me. Dusty Jones, whom I had seen at a couple of the open mats, walked over, stuck out his hand and introduced himself. He was one of the co-captains, and he welcomed me to the practice. Dusty told me that it was going to be a fun season, and offered to help me if I had any questions. I think a lot of the other guys saw this, and figured that if a senior co-captain talked to me, then I was pretty much off-limits from any teasing.

Coach Green began our first practice with a speech about his expectations. He told us not to focus on how demanding he was; he said the sport was more demanding than he could ever be. Coach Green spoke about the time required of us—there would be lengthy practices each day after school and also on Saturday mornings. He didn't waste a moment of that time, which I learned right away. After 15 minutes of stretching, we hit the mats, and paired off with guys of similar weights to wrestle for the next 90 minutes or so. It was a lot like open mats. I had a chance to work on moves, get a feel for how my body could bend and twist, and learn which muscles I could rely upon and which ones I needed to work on in the weight room.

At the end of wrestling, we did several conditioning drills, which was something I had never experienced before. In rapid-fire succession, we did sets of 50 push-ups, 50 sit-ups, and 50 squats. I did those exercises just like everyone else, because, except for the squats, legs were not needed. Sit-ups are easy to imagine. My abdominal muscles were the axis for movement in that exercise. When I did push-ups, I put my hands beside my chest, leaned with my face to the ground, and pushed my body up in the air. The rest of the guys put their toes on the ground to

Celebrating my fourth birthday during lunchtime at the preschool program at James Ryder Randall Elementary School. *Photo courtesy of Trevon Jenifer*

When I was four years old in 1992, my Christmas present was a power-wheeler, which my stepfather fixed so that I could control the power through a switch on the handlebars, and not the pedals on the floor. Here I am riding the bike outside our apartment in Suitland, Maryland. *Photo courtesy of Trevon Jenifer*

At age four, I was fitted for my prosthesis. Here I am at my Grandma Francine's house learning how to move in my new legs. I never really got the hang of it.

Photo courtesy of Trevon Jenifer

I was never bashful about trying new things in Mr. Gray's adapted physical education class at Randall— except for that big ball in the background. I was a little hesitant about climbing onto it, but I still tried to dribble it like a basketball.

Photo courtesy of Trevon Jenifer

Here I am in fourth grade. As I grew up, I tired of my prosthetic legs, which often didn't fit comfortably due to how fast I was growing.

Photo courtesy of Trevon Jenifer

Wheelchair track gave me my first chance not only to compete athletically, but also to do so against similarly determined people. Even though I often competed with and against older athletes, those experiences pushed me to stay at their level. It worked. I set several national records that still stand.

©1998, The Washington Post. Photo by Shawn Thew. Reprinted with permission.

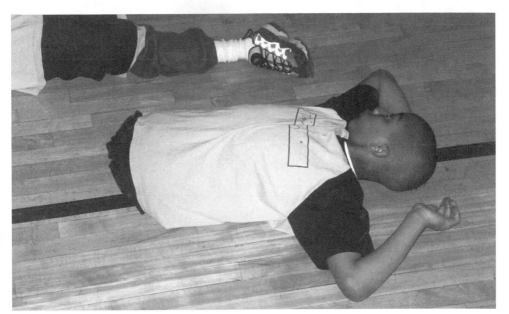

As a seventh grader at Kettering Middle School, I tried to stay active like other kids. P.E. gave me a good chance to stay in shape, especially after I decided to quit wheelchair sports. *Photo courtesy of Trevon Jenifer*

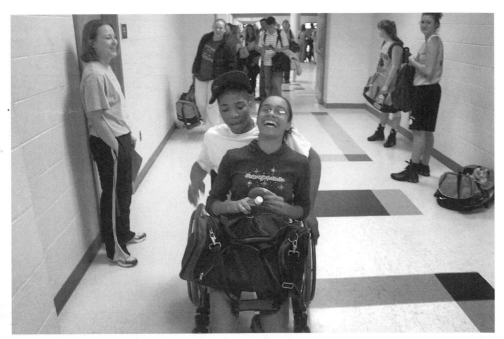

This was my home away from home—the hallway in between the wrestling room and the gymnasium at Huntingtown High School. Here I am during my junior year giving my friend Caroline Jones a ride in my wheelchair. These kinds of gestures helped me break the ice with my classmates, who were sometimes a little awkward about my condition. *©2005, The Washington Post. Reprinted with permission.*

You can see just how far my opponents had to bend over to be able to wrestle me. It left them a bit off-balance, which I tried to use to my advantage.
Photo courtesy of Huntingtown High School

Wrestlers are trained to go at their opponents' legs. That forced my opponents to attack me a little differently, while I had an eye-level shot of their legs.
Photo courtesy of Judy Smart

My arms and shoulders were much larger than those of my opponents. My few critics said it was unfair that I was so much stronger than my opponents. I wonder if those critics ever thought it was unfair that my opponents had legs.
Photo by Chris Lekhavanija

I'm on the verge of a pin here, and it's easy to see how. My opponent has no control over his arms or legs. Most wrestlers use their legs to tie up those of their opponents', while using their arms to control the upper body. I had to be more creative.
Photo courtesy of Judy Smart

Here I am on the way to my junior year Prom. Wrestling proved to be my way into Huntingtown High's social circle, as most of my classmates became very interested in my success. When I came home from Prom my senior year, I was wearing the King's crown. *Photo courtesy of Trevon Jenifer*

It was easy for me to smile for my senior portrait after everything I had accomplished in just two years at Huntingtown High School.
Photo by Lifetouch

For the people who told me years ago that I would never graduate from high school, here's my response. My family and friends were so proud of me, not only for this, but also for my desire to be the first person in my family to go to college. *Photo by Lifetouch*

stabilize the lower half of their bodies as they did each movement. I didn't have a lower body to stabilize. As a result, I did push-ups about twice as quickly as everyone else.

When it came time to do squats, which primarily strengthen legs, I eventually devised a way to make the exercise beneficial to my body. I stood upright, bent my elbows, and pushed myself skyward as my body—hands and all—lost contact with the ground. I came down with so much force, that I shot myself right back into the air. It almost felt as if the floor had springs when I did squats, and they gave my forearms and shoulders a good workout.

Practice ended with the part I dreaded the most—running. Even if the weather was warm enough for us to run outside, the track at Huntingtown had not been completed. Instead, we went upstairs to the second floor and ran laps around the rectangular hallways, which featured long straight-aways. I later found out that six laps around the floor were equal to one mile. Coach Green didn't tell us we had to run a certain distance, but we had to keep moving for 20 to 25 minutes.

That made me feel a little bit better, because there was no way I could keep up with the rest of the guys using my hands. I noticed this as soon as we started running. Even though Coach Green didn't expect me to do anything more than walk on my hands the way I always had—by putting my hands on the floor and swinging my body forward—I wanted to push myself. I went faster than I probably should have, not allowing myself rest in between each movement. I kept going, and by the time I completed three laps around the floor in about 15 minutes, my arms were killing me. They only hurt more as each wrestler ran past me, some of them several times.

Finally, Coach Green blew his whistle and announced it was the last lap for everyone. It didn't matter where we were on the floor; we were to finish once we hit the starting point. Once one person finished, he stood beside Coach Green and started clapping rhythmically. Everyone joined in the clapping once they finished. After about two minutes, I realized I was the last guy out there. I felt horrible. It was the first practice, and already I had stuck out in an unfavorable way. Never mind that there was no way anyone could have expected me to keep pace with the rest of the guys. But why couldn't I have been right by the finish line when Coach Green blew his whistle? That way I could have been one of the first guys to finish. Instead, I had two full hallways to go before the end.

My shoulders were burning with pain. This was a workout unlike any I had ever had. It couldn't end quickly enough. I wondered if I could make it. The hallways were between 50 and 70 yards, but at that moment, it felt like 50 or 70 miles. I made a right turn to the last hallway, and there at the end stood something I will never forget: 25 guys, plus Coach Green and his assistants, Bruce Bevard and Matt Bancroft, clapping furiously. "C'mon, Trey," I heard someone yell. "You can do it."

I was still in pain, but couldn't suppress the smile that came to my face when I heard the entire team cheering me on. I had just been through three hours of pure hell. I had put my body through the most rigorous training session I had ever endured. And I did it all in front of a bunch of guys who hardly knew me. To them, I thought, I was the black kid in the wheelchair who didn't have legs. But once again I was wrong. I might have been the only black kid there, and I certainly was the only one without legs. That, however, was secondary at that moment. I was their teammate, above all else.

I learned then that teammates do special things for one another because they wear the same uniform. They share in each other's emotions. When I hurt, they hurt. They wanted to see me finish almost as much as I wanted to finish. I couldn't believe this attachment, especially after just one practice. I had never shared this kind of bond with teammates in any other sport. It took a moment like this for me to understand what my stepfather had told me—that wrestling was a team sport. As I crossed the finish line, guys patted me on my back and told me they knew I would finish. They were encouraging, but not belittling, a fine line for me.

We were all tired. We all hurt. Everyone else knew, though, that this was the first time I had done something like this, and they wanted to give me confidence for the future. Each of them had struggled through a drill before. It was almost as if I had been initiated; I earned my letters when I crossed that line.

But my real induction came seconds later. Coach Green was proud of us for hanging in there the entire practice, and told us to get used to those sessions. It was his policy not to cut anybody. Every one of us, as long as we stayed with the program, would be guaranteed a spot on the varsity or the junior varsity team. The only way I wouldn't wrestle would have been if I chose to quit. I had made the team.

Coach Green told us that the only way the sport can grow was through participation, and cutting people would hurt that. I knew he also took pride in the sport because it taught its participants discipline. It was a vital trait we could all use long after we stopped wrestling, and something we didn't learn in any classroom.

My teammates' applause was the icebreaker I needed for conversation with the team. After that episode, I found myself much more relaxed and comfortable around my teammates. I tried to take advantage of each opportunity to tell a joke and lighten the mood. For example, during one practice, a bunch of guys came down with cramps in their legs. They sat against the wall and rubbed their calves to try to loosen them up and get back on the mat.

"Leg cramps are the worst," I said, looking over at them. "I get them all the time."

There were about two seconds of hesitation. Everyone looked around before the whole room burst out laughing. I've never had a problem with self-deprecating humor. It's a lot like comedians who make racial or ethnic jokes. If the comedian is a member of that group, then it's almost understood that it's okay for him poke fun. Nobody would dare come up to me and make a joke about me or some other person with a similar disability. But I could get away with it.

It wasn't until later that school year that I realized how those jokes helped me fit in at Huntingtown. Everyone felt like they were walking on eggshells around me, especially when they wanted to ask me something about my body. They all worried about choosing the perfect words to ask the question, for if they made the slightest misstep, they could have come across as rude or insulting. Luckily for them, I understood this. I knew they were curious, but uncomfortable. A joke—even at my own expense—was the perfect way to ease any awkwardness and open the door for other kids to ask me sensitive questions.

If only jokes could have eased my tension on the mat.

For three weeks, I went to practice, worked on developing my moves, learned the culture of the sport, and got to know my teammates. Yet I still had no idea if I was any good. We all practiced together, from the seniors, like Phil Riley, who had wrestled for more than half his life, to the freshmen and newcomers like me, who had never touched a wrestling mat before that fall. Everyone was going to get a uniform and wrestle that season; the only question was whether it would be for the varsity or junior varsity. There were moments when I impressed myself and felt comfortable with how quickly I had picked up the sport. But as soon as I got that feeling, I would make an amateur move and get pinned.

When I arrived at a Tuesday practice in early December, I saw a photographer outside the wrestling room. This was the day that each of Huntingtown's winter sports teams took their team pictures. I had seen what other teams did in the fall season when I looked through the fall sports program. The football team, for example, took several different photos—one for the varsity, another for the junior varsity, and a third for the freshman team. Coach Green wouldn't allow that. All 26 of us lined up for just one picture. He always preached that we were one team. It didn't matter if we competed separately, we were all part of Huntingtown wrestling. The goal was the same for everyone— make this the best wrestling program in the state. To some of the guys, gestures like that might have seemed pretty subtle, or been completely ignored. I saw this as another way to enhance the closeness of the team and make us all feel a part of something special.

Coach Green was good with clever touches like that. The previous weekend we had our only scrimmage, just up the road at Northern High School, where Coach Green had been an assistant for three years before he took the Huntingtown job. A few different teams were there. We didn't compete team against team. Instead, each wrestler was paired with a comparable opponent, so that each coach could gauge his wrestlers' abilities. Wrestlers were placed by their coaches into four different groups: beginners; those with a year or two of experience; those with two to three years of experience; and those who were wrestling "lifers." I was surprised when Coach Green put me in the second group, but I held my own in two matches there. Coaches didn't keep score; they just ran the clock for the usual three two-minute periods.

Several weeks later, I asked Coach Green why he put me in that group. He told me that there was no sense in pairing me with rookie wrestlers. Even though we would have had the same experience on the mat, they were completely unprepared to face someone like me. They were struggling enough just trying to learn the sport against two-legged opponents. The last thing they needed in their wrestling education was a new variable that they wouldn't encounter again. Coach Green figured I would have defeated those kids easily, and that would have given me a false impression of myself.

I made some solid moves at the scrimmage, but Coach Green told me that I left myself vulnerable to be put on my back too many times. I thought I was struggling. That was why Coach Green caught me off-guard when he told me at practice the following Tuesday: "Trevon, you're our 103 on varsity. Congratulations." I was stunned, but I really shouldn't have been. There were no other 103-pounders in the program, but I didn't know that. The only other person who could have done it was a freshman named Daniel Justice, who had been my practice partner several times. But Daniel was 113 pounds; there was no way he could make weight at 103. In fact, he would end up being our 112-pounder.

As we all cleaned up the wrestling room, rolled up the mats, and left school, I thought about what I had just accomplished in making varsity. I was going to represent my school and wear that Huntingtown uniform. I rolled in my wheelchair toward the parking lot, where my stepfather was waiting to take me home. Phil

Riley saw me get into the car and said, "First match, Trey, in two days. Be ready, man."

It was time to stop celebrating and start focusing.

I weighed 95 pounds then, so I was in a unique position. Unlike every other wrestler, I needed to gain weight instead of lose weight, and I did that as the season progressed. Coach Green told me that at 95 pounds, I sacrificed 10 percent of my body weight to my 103-pound opponents. My opponents had a huge advantage on me because I was lighter.

I still had a little bit of baby fat on me, partly because I had never worked out in a constant routine. When I was a sophomore at Central, I did exercises like the bench press and the rowing machine, but I went through phases. Sometimes, I lifted every day for a couple of weeks, and then I didn't touch a weight for a month. There was plenty of room for my body to fill out and my muscles to become toned, and that would help me, because muscle weighs more than fat.

Even though my arms and shoulders were much bigger than other 103-pounders, I still needed to get stronger because I didn't have leg muscles to help me. I realized how important it was for me to bulk up throughout preseason practice. Coach Green tried to teach me a couple of the moves he saw Kyle Maynard or other disabled wrestlers use effectively. We worked on one drill we called "The Fireman's Carry." I had to pick up another wrestler from his knees, and then swing him over my shoulders. I was able to pick up my opponent, but his body was so heavy that I had no command over holding him, and, ultimately, I always fell over. It was especially tough because there were no other 103-pounders on the team, so that meant I would have to carry someone heavier than me.

We also did wheelbarrow races as a drill. It was a little different with me, since I couldn't carry anyone's legs and walk at the same time. Instead, a teammate put his hands on the ground, rested his feet on my shoulders, and we ran about 60 yards down the hallway. I loved it when we switched positions. I was used to walking on my hands, and my teammate didn't have any feet to hold, so he just grabbed my hips. It looked a little funny, because this was the only time when the guy who was standing had to crouch down a bit in order to reach my hips. But it gave everyone a good laugh.

Coach Green and I were learning so much about what I could and couldn't do in terms of training. It reminded me a lot of working with Mr. Gray. Both he and Coach Green were creative and were curious to try things that might have seemed off the wall at first. But I was all for off the wall—the stranger the better. I didn't have a fear of failure, and neither did Coach Green. He treated me like everyone else, and that meant so much to me.

Coach Green never asked me, "Can you do this?" He knew how I hated to be singled out, and if he treated me one way, then he had to do the same for everyone else. I knew he wouldn't take it easy on me, and I loved that. Even if he didn't think about how it would make me feel, he knew it wouldn't be fair to the other kids. If he gave me half the work as everyone else, then I would be expected to perform half the job of everyone else.

And my teammates soon saw that I could perform beside them. Daniel Justice told me how I had great leverage because my center of gravity was at the middle of my chest. Everyone else's center of gravity was at the waist. Coach Green instructed me to lean forward with my head to guard against contact. That way, when an opponent pushed toward me, the bottom of my torso would slide backward, and I would land on my stomach and not my back. That helped to prevent me from being pinned, since wrestlers need to be on their backs in order to be pinned.

I had spent a lot of time and energy on the mat, learning to develop a strategy and plan of attack that was specific to me. I was anxious for our first match, but at the same time, I was so scared and nervous. From listening to my teammates and coaches talk to one another, I knew that I still had so much to learn. It wasn't that they talked about me, but they spoke about moves and positions that I still didn't understand. I asked Coach Green about this once, and he told me that even though I was so eager to take in all this new knowledge, I had to be patient and concentrate on the fundamentals. Patience wasn't always my strong suit, especially with my first match looming ahead.

8

Heading into my first match, my main concern was with how my opponents would approach me, and how I would respond. Everyone would soon find out just how good a wrestler I was—and no one was more interested in the answer than me. In my first match, I learned quickly that hesitancy wasn't going to produce results. I was all style—trying to dance around the mat in anticipation—but no substance. My lack of aggression hurt me, and I was pinned easily. In my second match, however, I focused on setting the tone and being the aggressor. The approach earned me my first pin and victory number one in my wrestling career.

The week after that first victory, word began to spread around school that the kid in the wheelchair was a wrestler. When people mentioned it, the natural response was, "Is he any good?" The bearer of news could then reply, "Yeah, he won his last match." Some people needed to hear that I won in order to pay me any notice.

It took a lot for wrestling to gain any attention among the student body. Even though it's a popular sport in Calvert County, it still couldn't capture the attention of non-partici-pants the way football or basketball did. The only students who went to matches were close friends of the wrestlers. The rest in attendance were either parents or wrestling junkies who were plugged into the sport's community and attended matches all over the state. There were kids who went to football games who didn't know the difference between a first down and a touchdown. A football game was as much a social scene as it was a spectator sport, because it was played on a huge field, outdoors, and on Friday nights. It started the weekend for everyone.

Wrestling matches couldn't compete with that. Everyone had to be inside the gymnasium, and weeknights weren't conducive to hanging out. Even worse were the tournaments, which were held on weekends. After Friday night's preliminaries—which were often scheduled at the same time as basketball games—Saturday's action usually began around 9 a.m., and the finals weren't completed until upwards of 12 hours later. It's common at a wrestling tournament to also have two different matches tak-ing place at the same time, so each match was competing against another for the crowd's attention.

Still, for my team's first match, the bleachers were packed with students, parents, some of the school's administrators, and even a reporter from the local weekly newspaper. I had never seen anything like this at a wheelchair track meet. The crowd at a football game may have dwarfed the number of folks packed into the gymnasium for that meet, but it was still a large enough audience to rattle my nerves.

My first victory lifted an enormous weight off of my shoulders. No longer did I have to prove to my teammates that I belonged. Even though they saw me work my butt off in practice and keep pace with them in every drill, exercise, and task Coach Green put in front of us, they never knew for sure how that would translate onto the mat when the season began. Now they knew that I could hold my own, which was a great feeling for me. But I had only two days to enjoy that victory. The following weekend, we headed to an 18-team tournament at Lackey High School. It would be the first chance for a lot of people to see me in action.

One of my matches was against a sophomore from Patuxent High School, Nick Damron, who had had no idea who I was. He asked around, and someone pointed him in my direction. From across the gym, he saw me sitting on a mat stretching, and thought my legs were just hidden by my seated posture. When it came time for our match that Saturday morning, Nick was stunned when I came onto the mat to shake his hand. He was completely unprepared for me, and it showed in the way he wrestled. He was very cautious, and it sort of reminded me of how my teammates treated me at the start of practice when they thought I was fragile.

I won the match, 11-10, and as I left the mat, a little girl of maybe eight or nine years old came running up to me. She told me her name was Tiffany.

"Can I have your autograph?" she asked, as she thrust a tournament program and a pen toward me.

I was sweating and out of breath from the match, but I was blown away by her request.

"I think you're amazing," she told me.

It was my first brush with fame, and I loved it. Tiffany's face is one that I will never forget. I never saw her again, and that has always bothered me. I put her alongside those people from Kettering, who said on that television piece about me that I was inspirational. Those were powerful words, and they never left me.

All the while, Nick, the wrestler I had just defeated, watched this exchange and laughed. He admitted to me that he had never seen anyone receive an autograph request at a high school wrestling tournament. But he also said he never met anyone like me. We sat in the bleachers and began to talk. Nick wanted to know everything about me—the origin of my condition, what my family was like, my background in Prince George's County, and why I took up wrestling. I was happy to talk to him, in part because the curiosity was mutual. He was a white kid who grew up in southern Calvert County, one of the county's last areas to be developed and suburbanized. I wanted to know about his life, too.

From that day, Nick and I developed a strong friendship. We wound up wrestling each other four more times that season, so we got used to seeing each other at meets and tournaments. I never really had friends on opposing teams when I competed in wheelchair sports, so this was a unique experience. It was also another instance of finding a friend in a place I least expected.

I finished sixth in that 18-team tournament. A few of my classmates, upon learning that I wrestled, were astonished that I could capably play a sport against two-legged opponents, and—given my victory—obviously do well enough to prove my spot on the team was no charity case. I was just as surprised by my success, but for a different reason. If someone had told me six months ago that I'd be a wrestler, I'd have thought they were crazy. And that's exactly what I told everyone who complimented me.

The most common question people asked me was, "How do you do it?" That question frustrated me so much because it seemed like they had given no thought to their question. I wanted to respond with, "How do *you* wrestle?" I know it was a cliché, and it bothered people to hear it, but I put on my singlet, got on the mat, and wrestled my opponent. How was that different from any other wrestler? I knew most teenagers wouldn't completely understand me when I told them that I didn't see myself as being "different." For people who rely on their eyes to make all of their observations, that's a very difficult concept to grasp.

But I was smart enough to know that I couldn't get away with that sort of defensive answer. It wasn't in my personality to snap at people. I had found my place in the school community by being warm and friendly, sort of following the cue given to me by Jessie and Alyssa. I didn't want to ruin almost four months of hard work trying to fit in just because a few people had asked me a thoughtless question. So my response was to give a confident answer: "I wrestle just like everyone else. Of course, I have an advantage in that they can't go for my legs." That answer drew plenty of laughs, but I could tell it didn't completely satisfy people's curiosity.

A few people had heard about Kyle Maynard's story, and, naturally, they asked me about him. They tried to draw comparisons between us, and asked me if I drew my motivation from him, or if it was he who inspired me to try wrestling. I smiled when they said that, and pleasantly told them that I had so much respect for Kyle, and thought what he did was exceptional. Deep down, though, I thought that people who compared us were pretty ignorant. Obviously, the only reason we were mentioned in the same breath was because we were missing limbs and chose to wrestle. It had nothing to do with how we wrestled. It's a lot like how people compared the music of Stevie Wonder and Ray Charles because they shared being blind and black. Anyone familiar with their music knew they each had a distinct sound.

Besides, early on in my wrestling career I wasn't someone who should have been compared to Kyle. I was inexperienced, and Kyle had advanced to the Georgia state tournament the previous year as a senior. How would that make Kyle feel, being compared to someone who had only won a couple matches? But regardless of my win total, I wanted people to see me for the *wrestler* I was, and not the unusual human body I had. I took pride in my aggressiveness on the mat and my dedication to learning a sport. Either of those were fine bases for comparison to another wrestler, or even another athlete. But I wanted to be treated as a wrestler first and foremost, not as someone with a disability.

When I told people that my athletic role model was LaVar Arrington, the star linebacker for the Washington Redskins at the time, many thought I was nuts. But I drew on the similarities between how intense we both were during competition. Sometimes when I watched Redskins games on television, I didn't follow the play, I just followed LaVar. He never stopped moving. He was always trying to make something happen, and that was what I told people I tried to do on the wrestling mat. I didn't think I was saying anything ridiculous. That was what I believed.

Crowds began to build at my matches after winter break. In early January we headed to Northern High School for another 18-team tournament. This was the first time I really noticed how much attention my matches were commanding. Word had spread throughout the area about me, and that I had already won a few matches. An Internet message board devoted to Maryland high school wrestling had plenty of discussions about me. I thought it was funny. Some of the responses suggested that I wasn't a real person, and that someone made up my story and posted it online as a hoax.

Very few people came to the preliminary rounds on Friday night, and I split my two matches that night. But by late morning Saturday, the gym was packed. Around noon, I had a match against a wrestler from Oxon Hill High School. I didn't know it at the time because I was so focused on my match, but people were so interested to watch me that they crowded around my mat shoulder to shoulder about two or three deep. One of my teammates told me that among the people watching were wrestlers from Parkdale High School. They were so interested in my match that they turned their backs to the gym's other mat just five feet behind them, where their teammate was wrestling.

The crowd eyed me intently, each person searching for the same answer: What was it that I did to compensate for not having legs? Showing them was much easier than telling them. My condition had forced me to develop certain muscles that most people aren't aware they even have. Each time I plant the palms of my hands on the floor to move my body, I essentially lift 100 pounds. That force puts stress on my hands, forearms, triceps, shoulders, and back. As a result, my arms are powerful and long, and my hands are enormous. From the tip of my middle finger to my wrist measures nine inches. That sort of length allows me to get a firm grasp on my opponents—most of which stand no taller than 5 feet, 4 inches—no matter where I grab onto them. My arm strength is enough to help break free if an opponent has his arms locked around me.

Perhaps the biggest advantage I have is the fact that my 103 pounds are packed into a much smaller body than my opponents'. I only have to spread that weight through my torso and arms, while my opponents have to distribute their weight between their legs, as well. As a result, my arms were much larger and stronger than my opponents'. Some other disabled wrestlers have been charged with having an unfair advantage because of this discrepancy of weight displacement. They've been accused of having arms that a 180-pound wrestler might have had he had legs. The claim was that it was unfair for them to wrestle against 103-pounders, who had to split their weight throughout a larger body. The best counter to that claim came from Nick Ackerman, a former 174-pound NCAA Division III champion. He lost both of his legs below the knees before he turned two years old due to bacterial meningitis. In an article, Ackerman claimed that nobody had told him he had an advantage when he had a losing record. Once he started winning, though, all of a sudden, it wasn't fair. Ackerman told his critics that if he had such an edge, then they should cut off their legs, too. It was hard for anyone to respond to that.

Coach Green prepared me for the fact that some of my opponents—fearing a no-win situation—might choose to forfeit to me, rather than get on the mat and wrestle me. This became a trend in wrestling once girls began to compete against boys in high school. Male wrestlers didn't want to face female opponents because a win wasn't considered an accomplishment since it was expected. But a loss brought with it a world of humiliation. It was easy for opponents to lump me into that same group. They knew they were supposed to beat me. How were they going to explain to their teammates that they lost to a guy with no legs? Coach Green told me that it would be easy for opponents to fake injuries to get out of matches against me.

I was actually surprised that none of my opponents ever tried to taunt me with slurs. I wasn't expecting any racial insults, since there were a handful of black wrestlers in Southern Maryland—a large enough number that we didn't feel completely alone. But there was nobody else like me, and so I worried that some of my opponents would stoop to calling me a "cripple" or teasing me about my condition. In a sport where every competitor seeks an edge whenever possible, I thought an opponent, maybe in a real moment of weakness, would resort to name-calling. It was smart of my opponents to resist; to do so would have only made me angrier and given me all the motivation I needed to defeat them.

If I had an edge at my second tournament of the year at Northern, it sure wasn't apparent. I wrestled like crap that weekend. The season was almost a month old, and I was worried that opponents had begun to figure me out, and I still didn't have a good sense of what I had to do to beat them. They were confused the first time they faced me, wondering, "How am I going to wrestle him?" Many of them actually backed up after the opening whistle instead of charging at me. Little did they know, that would have been their best move—to come right at me and knock me on my back, where I would have been virtually helpless. Instead, they crouched down, so as to get their eyes on an even level with mine, and also block me from going for their legs. By crouching over, however, they didn't realize that they were placing themselves in an off-balance position. At the time, however, I didn't notice these holes in the defense. I was still learning, too, after all. I played it cautiously, waiting for them to come at me.

My hesitancy cost me in my second match of the tournament against a wrestler from Surrattsville High from Prince George's County. Midway through the third period, he came at me near the edge of the circle and picked me up. We struggled for a couple of seconds, while I tried to break free, but ultimately, he slammed me down just outside the circle. I landed on my right shoulder with a loud thud that made Coach Green wince. The pain was unlike anything I had experienced. I rolled over onto my back and tried to lift my arm ever so slightly, but I couldn't. It felt like someone was stabbing at my shoulder.

This was a new feeling, since I had never been hurt before. When I competed in wheelchair sports, I never had anything worse than a cut happen to me. Probably the most traumatic episode came at a wheelchair track practice, when I was rolling down a hill by Roosevelt High School. It was a steep decline that caught me off-guard, and as I tried to slow down, I jerked the chair such that it threw me from my seat. I cut my elbow, but that was the extent of it. I had never put myself in a position where I could be out-muscled and pushed around—until I chose a contact sport like wrestling. My opponent's move wasn't illegal or dirty, I just wasn't ready for it.

I heard my mother screaming in the background as I lay on the mat. This was the one thing that bothered her the most about wrestling. She had always been very overprotective of me, which stemmed from the days right after I was born. Throughout my childhood, almost every one of my physical activities made her tense. Even worse, my mother knew nothing about the sport, and she became immediately concerned during the first match she watched due to all the tugging, clutching, and brute force of the wrestlers.

Coach Bancroft left his seat in the coach's corner and hurried toward me to see if I needed any help. I waved him off and told him I would finish the match. But a medical trainer was already on her way over to me. She massaged my shoulder, and noticed, "Wow, that's a big bump you've got." Coach Green was there to respond: "That's not a bruise. That's his muscle." I smiled and got up to finish the match, which I lost, 8-2. I shook hands with my opponent and scurried off the mat to the nearest wall. I leaned up against it, crying as I held my shoulder. I spent the rest of the evening in my wheelchair with an ice pack on my shoulder while I watched my teammates' matches.

I was just a month into the wrestling season, and I knew people were watching every move I made. That was why I turned away Coach Bancroft's offer to help me up. I was so committed to proving my strength and fortitude that I was probably in danger of hurting myself even more by trying to show how tough I was. When it came time to board the bus back to school later that night, someone tried to help me out of my wheelchair and onto the bus. I swatted his hand away and fired a glare that said his offer was almost insulting. But it wasn't. I was just too stubborn to accept that it was okay to depend on others for help. I should have been thankful for the helping hand.

I split the six matches I wrestled in that weekend, and finished in sixth place in the tournament after losing to my friend Nick Damron in the fifth-place match. That left my record for the season at 8-7, a mediocre mark that didn't impress me at all. But apparently it caught the attention of others. A reporter and a photographer from *The Washington Post* had been following me for about a week. The reporter met me two weeks earlier when I was at school, watching a basketball game during winter break. He was intrigued by my story—not only with my decision to wrestle, but also how I was able to blend into a new, and much different, community late in my childhood. The reporter and photographer followed me through a day in school, and watched me at practice and on my way home. They watched how I interacted with other kids, like how I used my wheelchair to give girls rides in the hallways after school.

After all of the time they spent with me, I was pretty excited to see what kind of story would appear in the paper. I showed up for school on Tuesday, January 11, 2005, and as I walked into my first class of the day, a classmate came up to me holding a copy of the *Post's* Sports section. "Can you autograph this?" he asked me. I couldn't believe it. On the top half of the front page of the section was this enormous photo of me lined up with my teammates just before a match. I was on the floor amongst several of my teammates, but the photo was taken in such a way that you couldn't see my teammates' faces, only their bodies from the chest down. The photo emphasized how much my teammates towered over me, which made for a startling photograph and showed people who had no knowledge about wrestling what I was up against. Beneath my story was a small photo of Indianapolis Colts quarterback Peyton Manning, who had just been named the NFL's Most Valuable Player. I joked to my friends later on, "I'm bigger than the NFL MVP."

As I went from class to class, teachers and classmates— some of whom I had never spoken to before—yelled out to me in the hallways. "Hey, congratulations. I saw you in the paper today." During several of my classes, my teachers read the story aloud, and everybody applauded me. I was kind of embarrassed, but also proud. If there was any doubt as to whether I fit into the Huntingtown community, that day erased it all.

Coach Green received a phone call that day from Ken Horsmon, the Superintendent of Calvert County Public Schools. Horsmon couldn't help but think about how the story might evolve. "You know," Horsmon told Coach Green, "I think we might get some serious press out of this." He was already too late. By the end of the school day, there were calls to the main office from three radio stations and three television stations. It continued over the next couple of weeks. *The Today Show* sent a reporter to one of my home meets, where I won both of my matches. Radio stations called from as far away as New Orleans and Salt Lake City.

All the media exposure gave people a chance to see how I went about my daily business. I woke up every morning at 5:15 and took my dog, a boxer named Sheba, out for a walk. My parents didn't excuse me from the same chores expected of other teenagers. If I didn't do my chores the previous night, I had to do them in the morning. On the weekends, I did laundry and tended to the flowerbeds beside the garage at our house. In the fall, I raked the leaves in our yard and put them into bags. I mopped the kitchen and bathroom by grabbing the mop with one hand, and pushing myself along the floor with the other. Maybe it took a while, but my mother always loved to brag to people, "That boy can clean a house." Of course, I liked to hold that over her head every time I needed money to go out with my friends.

I was just as hard-working when it came time to help out the wrestling team. Whenever we had a home match, we had to clean up the gym afterwards. While my teammates rolled up the mats, I took the folding chairs used to line the mats for the team benches, and placed them on the seat of my wheelchair as I rode around the gym toward a storage closet. I refused to be held to a different standard than everyone else, so I made sure my contributions were significant.

Meanwhile, Coach Green fielded all of the calls and responded to messages, and that put him in a tough position. He knew how much I loved the attention and how I enjoyed talking to people. He didn't want me to miss any opportunity to enjoy the exposure and perhaps use it to open doors to other athletic or educational chances elsewhere. But he also knew the cold reality that because I looked different, people could use that to exploit me as joke. Five minutes of laughs for them, Coach Green said, could turn into a lot of humiliation for me.

He also warned me of the questions reporters wanted to ask me, and he was right. A lot of them wanted to dramatize my life by telling their audience what I couldn't do, rather than what I could. Coach Green always told me to be proud of what I could do, and his pride was obvious in how hard he worked to teach me how to wrestle. He told me from the start that he threw out the book on Wrestling 101 when it came to coaching me. Instead, he learned new things on his own, and he said how much he enjoyed that process. It energized him as a coach, because it introduced him to a completely new way of thinking.

Not every person who called to speak with me was a member of the media. One day during wrestling practice, our vice principal took a message for me from a man who wanted to speak to me. It's unfortunate that he never called back, because the man was LaVar Arrington, the football player I had named as my role model in the *Post* article. Someone with the Redskins had shown him the article, and LaVar wanted to speak to me. Our vice principal didn't want to pull me out of wrestling practice, so she just asked LaVar to call back. She didn't realize how unlikely it would be that an NFL player would have the time to call back. I still think about how amazing it would have been to talk to him, but maybe I'll get my chance one day.

But most of the phone calls were from reporters, many of whom liked to ask me a lot of hypothetical questions. The one that bothered me the most was, "What if you had legs?" That had to be the silliest question anyone could have asked me, and I was sure they would have realized that after they spoke to me for five minutes. Asking me to consider life with legs was like asking, "What would happen if the sun rose in the West?" Both were pointless questions. I was the person I was because I didn't have legs. If I had legs, then maybe I would have become a basketball player, or maybe a world-class chess player, or maybe the brightest scientist the world had ever known. Or maybe I wouldn't have found success like I had in my life, because I wouldn't have embraced challenges. It was an impossible question to answer.

Another question I heard a lot from the wrestling community was, "How good would you be if you had started as a high school freshman, if not earlier?" Even I thought about that a little bit, especially as I won three matches in a row—none by forfeit—to end the month of January and run my record to 15-12. I was stunned by my success. Given how slowly I had taken to the sport during the preseason practices and open mats, I figured wrestling was going to take plenty of time to master, and I would have a losing record as a result. It wasn't like wheelchair track or even any of exercises Mr. Gray devised for me when I was younger. In both of those settings, I had no opponent who could affect me while I competed. In wrestling, I could have faced a state champion, who would have turned me into mincemeat. But I also could have been matched up with a guy who was on the mat for the first time, and like many of my opponents that season, looked at me, and then looked at his coach like a deer in headlights, with a face that screamed, "What do I do here?"

I talked with my stepfather about that one night. If I had started wrestling earlier, would I have been a state-championship contender by my junior year? I wanted to think that would have been the case, but he gave me an interesting perspective. He suggested that I had an added drive to succeed because I only had two years to complete my high school wrestling career, while everyone else had four. I had a lot to accomplish in that time, he said.

I took that attitude with me into the postseason: work hard and work fast, because time wasn't on my side. Coach Green never had to worry about keeping me motivated. It was hard to talk about matches after I lost, because I was always so angry about losing. I didn't throw tantrums or act like a sore loser, but after each loss, Coach Green knew that I wanted no part of anyone until I cooled down. I may not have known what move to make in the middle of the match, when I ultimately lost the decisive points. Once the final horn sounded, though, I knew exactly how and when I screwed up. Coach Green and I talked about the match in depth the following day, when we watched the video of the match after practice.

My goal was to qualify for the state tournament that season, but first, I needed to qualify for the regional tournament. From there, the top four finishers advanced to the state tournament. In order to qualify for the regional, I needed to place high enough in the Southern Maryland Athletic Conference tournament to amass enough rating points. Coach Green figured it would take a fourth-place finish to do that. When I lost again to my friend Nick Damron, 11-6, in the semifinals of the consolation round, I lost my chance to place high enough. I lost my last match of the tournament, 6-2, to Jake Shilling of La Plata High School, and finished sixth in the tournament. My season was over with a record of 17-18.

I wasn't upset, though, which surprised me. I was able to step away and look back on the season and realize how much I had accomplished in such a short amount of time. I could measure my accomplishments in the same way I grasped Mr. Gray's tasks at Randall. I didn't have any tournament titles or a flashy record to tout, but I was able to look at myself on that February evening and be content with my short wrestling career. I went from having never touched a wrestling mat six months earlier to winning 17 matches in a conference that had produced 31 individual state champions in the previous 25 years.

I didn't want the wrestling season to end, so I continued to go to practice the following two weeks as some of my teammates prepared for the regional and, ultimately, state tournaments. I used the time to work on more of my moves, but also to watch guys like our team captain, Phil Riley, and see how they trained for the most important matches of their lives. Phil didn't have to work hard; he already had his football scholarship to Hofstra, and he had fulfilled all of his graduation requirements. All he had to do was coast through the final four months of school. But that wasn't in his nature. I admired his determination and commitment. I wanted to be in his position the following year—wrestling for a state championship.

Coach Green saw that drive in me, as I kept returning to practices, even though other wrestlers, whose seasons had ended, did not. The week before the state tournament, some of the teams in Southern Maryland—like Huntingtown, Calvert, and Northern—practiced together since they had so few wrestlers left in the tournament. I tagged along, hoping to see some of Southern Maryland's best wrestlers in action. It only helped me to practice and watch these guys.

Coach Green rewarded me for my dedication; he asked me to come with Huntingtown's state-qualifying wrestlers to Cole Field House at the University of Maryland for the two-day Maryland State Tournament. I remember how intimidated I was for my first home match, when there might have been 200 people in the bleachers at Huntingtown. When we arrived at Cole Field House, there were wrestlers, coaches, parents, and friends representing the 136 schools that had tournament qualifiers. It was an amazing scene. There were eight mats stripped across the floor of the arena—four of them dedicated to the state tournament for the small schools, and the other four for the large schools. By Saturday night, a few thousand of the seats were filled for the championship matches. We all went crazy when Phil won the heavyweight title against a guy he had lost to in the regional final the previous weekend. I had never seen Phil so happy before, but I was also glad to know that I had watched him so carefully all season. I had studied a state champion, and at the very least, Phil provided a road map for me to get there myself.

Phil drove me home from the state championship, and the hour-long drive took me back to that night three months earlier when I won my first match. We talked about what an amazing atmosphere it was in that arena.

"You know, you can get there," Phil told me.

"You think so?" I asked.

"You saw those 103s," Phil said, speaking of the wrestlers in my weight class. "They've been wrestling for years. You just started, and look where you are."

9

It's a hard job being the most popular kid in school. I know that sounds like Miss America complaining about how hard it is being beautiful, but there's a difference. Beauty doesn't require responsibility. Of course, it was a responsibility I brought upon myself. And after wondering if I would ever fit in at my new school, I was so glad that I had done just that, and more.

By the end of wrestling season, I was the one kid everyone knew at Huntingtown. It was hard not to notice me, but not just because of my disability. Between my classes, wrestling practice, and hanging out afterwards, I was at school for close to 11 or 12 hours each day. Some kids called me Mr. Huntingtown, because I was in the building more often than my own house. Six months into the school year, I had found a home there.

Wrestling had not only proven to be a great way to make friends with my new teammates, it also turned out to be the perfect conversation starter with my classmates. They were able to initiate things with me by congratulating me on a recent victory, or by asking me about what happened at the previous night's meet. I knew most of the kids didn't know—or even care—much about wrestling, but I knew my story intrigued them because it transcended the sport. All it took was a couple of sentences of wrestling small-talk, before I made sure the conversation veered toward a more general discussion, and we could talk about things we both had in common. I had to laugh at that. Just a few months before, I thought I shared nothing with these kids. But I learned that we could both relate to anything that happened inside that school building.

In late October of my junior year, the school's fire alarms sounded. We were having our first fire drill. Everyone in Mr. Johnson's math class lined up by the doorway and proceeded toward the staircase. I was in my wheelchair.

"I guess I can't take the elevator, right?" I asked Mr. Johnson.

"That's okay," he said. "I'll carry you."

"What do you mean?" I laughed. "I'll walk downstairs."

"You'll *what?*"

I got on my hands and went downstairs like I had done since I was toddler. That day, I went so quickly, I beat Mr. Johnson to the front of the school, where the rest of the students met up.

"You've got to be kidding me," he said when he found me with the rest of our class. "The next time we have a fire drill, you're going to be the one carrying me on your shoulders."

Whenever I was in the hallways, either in between classes or hanging out after school, I had to say hello to anyone who made eye contact with me. That goes with the turf of being Mr. Popular. The problem with that was, I needed to remember everyone else's name, and that's was tough because I have a terrible memory. If someone said hello to me and I didn't reply by acknowledging them, then they often figured that there must be something wrong. Was I angry with them? Before the end of the next period, there would be a rumor going around that I was having a fight with someone. Girls, especially, would flip out on me if I forgot their name, or if one of them said hi as they walked past me in the hallway and I didn't respond, even if I was talking to someone else. It was all in good fun, but I got a lot of heat from people when I didn't say hello.

Someone once jokingly asked me if there was a person in the school that I didn't know, or with whom I wouldn't speak. I talked to everyone—guys, girls, jocks, nerds, white kids, black kids, seniors, freshmen, loud and expressive kids, quiet and shy kids. There were days I didn't eat lunch, but it wasn't because I didn't have money. I just spent the entire period hopping from table to table talking to different groups of people. High school is all about cliques, but I tried to stay away from that. To me, cliques enable kids to stay separated, and that was something I learned to hate early in my life at Randall. Cliques single people out, often based solely upon appearance. I would look at the jock clique, and ask myself why those kids didn't hang out with non-athletes. At best, the jocks were being ignorant, thinking that they didn't have anything in common with the non-athletes. At worst, they thought they were better than everyone else, just because of the way they looked or dressed. Regardless, those were two attitudes I had spent my whole life fighting against.

When I began going to open mats, I still wasn't sure whether I would stick with wrestling. So I looked for other social outlets at the same time, in case wrestling didn't work out. I asked my government teacher, Mary Casey, in late September, about joining student government, which she supervised. I figured that was an activity open to all students, and it encouraged everyone to interact with each other. It was good way to meet people.

"What can I do to help?" I asked her after class one day.

"Well, we've got Homecoming in a month, and we need all the help we can get," she replied.

The Homecoming committee met twice a week to prepare for the event. It was a little strange because it was a first-year school, so nobody really came home. Homecoming, though, is such an important part of the high school experience, and Huntingtown needed that. School officials thought about calling it a "Welcoming" instead, but they later thought that it wouldn't attract people the way "Homecoming" would.

I volunteered for everything, even though I was assigned to do tasks that didn't involve moving around. When it came time to decorate the gymnasium for the Homecoming dance, I wanted to show off a little bit. I hung signs and ribbons to the walls. I think I surprised some people by moving so quickly up the bleachers to tape things onto the wall. We wrapped up everything just in time, though it was a pretty frantic few days. When we finished, Ms. Casey asked us all when we expected to arrive at the dance. I told her I didn't think I was going to come, but she insisted that I attend. After all, she said, I worked on the committee and that earned me a free ticket. I couldn't say no.

The dance was a great scene, even if it was a little crowded. The entire school was there, and it really gave me a sense of community I hadn't felt before, certainly not at Central. I had a fun time being around everyone, and receiving congratulations for setting up the gymnasium. It was another step in my effort to blend in with the rest of the student body. When people asked me silly questions about the amazing things I did, they wouldn't consider decorating a gymnasium on that list. It didn't showcase my strength, mobility, or independence. They wanted to hear about me running laps on my hands or climbing stairs. But those were activities I did on my own. Working on Homecoming, however, allowed me to take part in something very important to the school community. I remembered how the students became so excited the week of Homecoming, and I told Ms. Casey that I wanted to remain a part of student government, even though wrestling conflicted with it for much of the winter.

When preparations for Homecoming came up the following year, I jumped into the planning right away. By that time, I was very popular at the school. Ms. Casey named me one of the three emcees for the Pep Rally held in the gymnasium the afternoon before the Homecoming football game later that night. The whole school packed into the gymnasium, and I helped lead the activities. As the assembly went on, the students grew louder and rowdier. It was all building up to the end, when the Homecoming Court was to be announced. I took turns with the two other emcees as we went through each class, naming that class' royalty. Finally, we made it to the seniors, and Samantha Watters announced those names.

Before the Pep Rally, I met with the two other emcees in the library to map out a plan for the assembly. Ms. Casey gave us each two pages of our responsibilities, and at the bottom were the names we were each supposed to announce for the Homecoming Court. Samantha showed me the senior class; I was voted Homecoming King. But I wasn't supposed to know that, and as we went into the gymnasium, I struggled to contain my excitement.

People told me all week that I was going to be named King, and I thought it was funny. Each class voted on its Homecoming Court, and I was one of five guys nominated to be King, so I knew it was a possibility. Still, the Homecoming King is usually regarded as the representative of the school. Imagine if someone who had never set foot in Calvert County came to Huntingtown and wanted to know what the place was all about. They would meet the Homecoming King because he was supposed to characterize the entire student body. I knew I could probably win a popularity contest with the rest of the students, but I didn't know if they would see me as someone who they could point to as the person who stood for everything Huntingtown.

I put on a pretty good act when Samantha called out my name to the crowd. I dropped my jaw, put both hands on my cheeks, and shook my head in disbelief. Everyone was cheering, even the teachers. I received another great response later in the night when the same processional was held on the football field, and I rolled out in my wheelchair to accept the Homecoming King's crown. I wore that all night through the dance.

When I considered what this recognition meant to me, I was overtaken with a remarkable feeling. Just a year earlier, I was a stranger to everyone in the school, except for my little brother. I knew nothing about the Calvert County community, and I honestly wasn't very thrilled to be a part of it. I didn't look like any of the other students, nor did I experience the childhood any of them had. My family was not as financially comfortable as the others in the community. My identity had almost nothing in common with anyone else's at that school.

It helped, though, that Huntingtown High School had no real identity itself when I arrived, because it was a first-year school. The rest of the student body drew from three different schools, and each one had its own distinct character. The cliques from each of those schools had a couple of kids who thought they were going to come to Huntingtown and own the place by making it a new version of their old school. That wasn't going to work, and it took a while for everyone to cut the cord from their old school and come together at Huntingtown. That allowed someone like me, who had no ties to any of those schools, to help shape the identity and be a unifying force for the student body.

Thinking about things in those terms, it made sense that I was named Homecoming King.

A wrestling tournament is like a game of survival, and it isn't just that way for the wrestlers. That's true of the fans, too. Beginning on a Friday night, the tournament concludes on Saturday, often lasting more than 12 hours that day before all the champions are crowned. Everyone looks at the people sitting beside him or her in the gymnasium bleachers as friends for the day. Of course, when I started to see the same people at our tournaments, those friendships became stronger than just day-long relationships. I got to know the parents and siblings of my teammates really well, because our team would stake out a section of the bleachers, and that was where the whole Huntingtown contingent stayed all day long.

I grew close to everyone who supported our team. When none of my teammates were wrestling, we really didn't pay attention to the matches going on, unless someone knew he was going to face the winner of a particular match. Sean DeVore was our 189-pounder when we were both juniors. He liked to wear a big cowboy hat and listen to country music, two things I wouldn't be caught dead doing. Still, we became good friends at practice. Sean was impressed with me right away, and he told his sister Katie, who was a sophomore, about me after the first couple of practices. Sean said he was amazed by my work ethic, and how

I managed to get along with everyone on the team. Katie humored her brother and listened. "Oh, and get this," Sean told his sister. "He doesn't have legs."

That jarred Katie's attention. She and Sean always supported one another with their activities—Katie with Sean's football and wrestling, and Sean with Katie's softball games in the spring. I always marveled at that because I had never had that type of relationship with any of my brothers or sisters. Katie took a great interest in my wrestling and sat beside the mat for each of my matches. She and I started talking at wrestling meets and tournaments, and we both felt very comfortable discussing anything. It was through Katie that I first saw how girls were able to open up to me and trust me with their emotions. A lot of girls told me I was a good listener and a trustworthy friend.

But I was intimidated by relationships. Dating was never easy for me. As much as I've tried to tell myself that not having legs doesn't make a difference, I can't convince myself that girls don't think about that when they look at me. While I was able to show a kindness and warmth that girls appreciated, I knew many of them wondered what they would miss out on in a relationship with me that they could get with normal guys. I can't hold a girl's hand while we're walking down the street or the school hallway. When it was time for me to dance with Blaine Hagler, the Homecoming Queen, it was a little awkward. I sat in my wheelchair, while we held hands and swayed back and forth for a while, before the rest of the party joined us on the dance floor. She wasn't intimidated by it and handled it very well, but when girls dream of being Homecoming Queen, that's not the kind of dance they envision. I just didn't feel like I was very appealing to teenage girls.

About two weeks before I graduated from Kettering Middle School, I heard from a couple of friends that a girl in my class had liked me. I thought they were joking with me. She was really cute, and could have had her choice of any guy in our class. There was no way she wanted to be with me. But my friends told me it was true. So I built up the courage to ask her. It turned out she did like me, and when I asked why she never said anything about it, she told me she was afraid to talk to me about it. It was the end of the school year, and we missed our chance to go out. That episode hurt me for a long time, but forced me, in the future, to be open with my emotions toward girls.

In some matters, though, I couldn't force the conversation. Three months into my junior year was the first time someone at Huntingtown asked me the question *everyone* wanted answered, but was too afraid to ask: "Well, do you have a, you know?" I do. I can have children. I go to the bathroom like all other guys. In fact, when I wore my prosthesis, there was a little hole cut out in the front. It allowed me the chance to urinate while standing up. The question came up every now and then throughout my childhood, and I understood why. It's difficult to tell whether or not I have a penis, even though I wear a Spandex uniform when I wrestle.

I'll never forget the first time I was asked that question. I was in sixth grade at Randall, and was getting a drink from a water fountain outside the bathroom. One of my friends was talking to me, and before I knew it, she asked me, "Can you have kids?" Guys started asking me that question in middle school, and I thought it was so funny watching them struggle to ask it. Not only was it a question most people never figure they'll have to ask someone, but 11- and 12-year-old boys are just about to hit puberty, and they are so confused about their own bodies, let alone someone else's.

People wonder how I don't hurt myself by moving around on the ground. The easiest answer I can give is that God must have understood how I was going to have to move around, and made sure it did not hang from the bottom of my body. When I slide along the floor, the bottom of my hip sockets is what touches the ground. Nothing else.

Throughout wrestling season, Katie told me I should return the favor during softball season and spend time at her games; she suggested I be the team's manager. There were a lot of girls I knew on the softball team besides Katie—like one of the team's captains, Kelli Seger, who had taken me to parties and been protective of me much like Moo—so I decided to give it a shot. I had never watched a softball game before, but what did I have to lose? When I told my stepfather that I wanted to be the softball manager, he was all for it.

The softball players were very close to one another. Just like the wrestlers, they had played together in local leagues throughout their childhood, and many of them were teammates on travel teams in the summer. After games and practices, they usually went out to eat or hang out. On one April afternoon, Katie was leaving practice with Jordon DeGennaro, our freshman catcher, and Brittany Norton, our senior first baseman. They saw that I was the last person from the team at school. I was waiting for my stepfather to pick me up on his way home from work.

"We're going to get a bite to eat," Brittany said. "You wanna come along?"

Brittany and I had never hung out before, and that was strange, because I thought we had a lot in common. She was very outgoing, and didn't mince words. Her car was bright orange, which fit her personality. She was just the kind of friend I was looking for. Brittany and I got along so well because she asked me questions. She was the first friend I met at Huntingtown who wasn't hesitant around me. She's not one for dead moments of silence, so she always talked about whatever was on her mind.

I often made it very clear that I understood people are curious about me, and Brittany caught on quickly that I would rather she ask me something, instead of wondering and remaining uninformed. One time, when I was at her house, Brittany watched me walk on my hands, and asked how I learned to move that way. I looked at her, confused.

"No, listen to me," she said. "Most babies, they first learned to roll around on the floor. Then they learn to crawl. Then they stand, and finally they take their first steps. What did you do?"

Nobody had ever asked me that, and that's precisely the kind of question I'm sure would intrigue almost everyone. Brittany thought about those kinds of things. Instead of highlighting the things I did that nobody else could, Brittany was more interested in discovering parallels between my life and hers. I always wanted people to view me as an equal, and that was exactly what Brittany did right off the bat.

Brittany never saw me as different, and she felt very strongly about that. We were in a mall one day, and there were a group of girls walking behind us. We saw one of them point to me, and say to her friends, "Oh my God, are you kidding me? Is he for real?"

Brittany stopped, turned around, and cocked her head.

"Excuse me?" she said.

The girls toughened their stance a bit. I grabbed Brittany's hand, and told her, "Calm down. It doesn't bother me. I've gotten used to it."

As we walked away, Brittany turned to me and said, "You might be used to it, but I'm not. That was rude."

When Brittany, Katie, and Kelli stood up and protected me, and invested their emotions in me, the least I could have done was support them on the softball field. I stayed with the team all season, and went with them to all of their games. It was a great time. The softball team lost just once and won the state championship. It was the first time a first-year school had won a softball state title in Maryland history, and it was a great source of school pride. Besides the friendship, I have another way to remember that season—the size 13 1/2 state championship ring I wear on my right hand. The players insisted I get one, too. They all agreed I was as much a part of the team as anyone in uniform.

I didn't think my 17-18 record as a junior was too impressive, especially to people who knew their wrestling. But apparently, the National Wrestling Hall of Fame thought differently. Our team was sitting in the stands at Cole Field House at the state championship meet, when a representative from the Hall of Fame's Maryland Chapter approached Coach Green. They wanted to nominate me for induction. Occasionally, the chapter honored a wrestler with a Medal of Courage, and they were considering me as a recipient.

To be considered for a hall of fame was pretty humbling. Just six months earlier I had never tried wrestling, and now I was being considered for recognition among the best in the sport. When they called Coach Green in September to tell him that I was inducted, I was thrilled. The induction ceremony was held at a hotel ballroom in Annapolis, Maryland. My whole family came to the ceremony, along with Coach Green, Mr. Taylor, and a couple of my teammates. Coach Green saved me again; he suggested I wear a tie to the ceremony, but neither my parents nor I knew how to tie one. Coach had a big smile as he put one on for me in the hotel lobby.

There were five former coaches who were inducted that day, and they each gave a long speech reflecting on their careers.

When they asked me to come to the podium and accept my honor, I knew I didn't have a lifetime of wrestling accomplishments. I thanked my family, Coach Green, and my teammates, and gave the only words of wisdom I felt comfortable saying.

"By getting this award," I told the audience, "I hope it will lift people to push harder and strive to get that extra yard."

And with that said, I knew I had several yards to gain myself. Practice started later that week, and I had big goals for my senior season.

I n the summer between my junior and senior years, I received a new mode of transportation that made it easier for me to get around. Dr. Herbert Goller, who made and adjusted my prosthesis, had retired and turned his business over to his son, Pete, who had a marvelous idea. Pete saw how restless and active I was, and knew that it was difficult to maneuver my wheelchair from place to place, especially in crowds or on bumpy ground. Anytime I got into a car, it was a big production having to fold up the wheelchair and sometimes it wouldn't fit. I told Pete how comfortable I feel walking on my hands, and that I preferred to get around that way.

Pete devised the perfect tool for me. He made a duplicate of the bucket that was attached to my prosthetic legs. But instead of fastening legs to the bottom of the bucket, Pete put the bucket on an 18-by-18-inch square board made out of hard plastic.

On the bottom of the board, he attached four wheels. It was like a skateboard, but I called it my scooter. I would sling my backpack over my shoulders and glide down the school hallways, sidewalk, or parking lot behind school. All it needed from me was a little push on the ground.

I rarely used my wheelchair once I got my scooter, and that hurt my ability to flirt a little bit, because I used to offer girls a ride down the school hallway on my wheelchair. But I could live with that. My scooter allowed me to go places my wheelchair often couldn't, and I'm grateful to Pete for his vision to create that.

Despite the progress I was making in my life, I received a rude awakening during the start of my senior year. My stepfather's mother had been diagnosed with breast cancer in January 2005, and by the summer, it had spread and attacked much of her body. She was in and out of the hospital before she died on September 5, 2005, two days before my 17th birthday. It really upset my stepfather, and it pulled him away from me for much of the year.

She had lived with her mother—my stepfather's grandmother—in a house in Fort Washington, which was about a half-hour north in Prince George's County. My great-grandmother relied on her daughter for her care, and with her gone, she needed my stepfather to provide that. Since her house was about 15 minutes from the car dealership where my stepfather worked, he began to stay there. The house was also closer to the drug store where my mother worked, and she stayed there, too. As a result, I was left at home with Jamar, and we took care of ourselves. My parents would stop by once a week to pick up clothing for themselves, drop off money and groceries for Jamar and me, and talk to us briefly.

While I missed my parents, I learned to become more responsible without them. I treated it as training for when I would have to live on my own. I had to cook my own meals, budget the food and money they gave me to last the entire week, and maintain a clean house. It meant a lot to me that my parents put that sort of trust in me, but it came at the expense of not having them around when I needed to talk with them. Jamar and I weren't particularly close, and if I needed some guidance with homework or something at school, I couldn't go into the next room and ask my parents. Their support just wasn't the same when it came over the telephone.

I didn't hold any grudges, though. My parents were there for me for 17 years and gave me the special attention I needed, even though they had six other children between them, and didn't want any of them to feel slighted. I wanted to make my senior year of school the most memorable of my life. I had dreams of going to college, and there was a lot of work to do. Neither of my parents had gone to college, nor did any of their other children. So I just don't think they understood what I was preparing to myself to do. Without my parents' close contact, times were tough.

Yet they continued to support me to the best of their ability. My stepfather, and usually my mother, always found time to make it to each of my wrestling matches. They saw how happy wrestling made me and how responsible it was for making me feel comfortable at Huntingtown, so they thought that was something they had to share with me. If they were preoccupied with family matters when it came time for schoolwork, then I had to find other people to help me make my senior year unforgettable.

I wound up doing a lot of that on my own.

"Trevon," Coach Green said, pulling me aside, "get in the middle with Curk."

That's how I found out I had been named team co-captain— along with Curk Smart, our 145-pounder—for my senior year. It was the beginning of our first practice on November 15, 2005, and everyone had just piled into the wrestling room to start our warm-up stretches. The captains always led those exercises by sitting in the center of the mat with the rest of the team surrounding them.

I tried to keep a stern look, and show the rest of my teammates that it was time to get serious, but it was tough to do. I had to bite my lower lip to keep from smiling ear to ear. Just as the Homecoming King was supposed to be representative of the school, the captain was whom the rest of team aspired to emulate. Only a year earlier, I had looked around that same room as a novice and wondered what to do and whom to follow. I thought about Phil Riley, one of our captains during my first year, and how I looked to him for guidance and support. Now, there were other guys looking at me the same way. It meant so much to me, but it also placed a lot of pressure on me. Phil was gone, as were the other seniors. It was time for me, Curk, and the three other seniors to pick up the slack. That wasn't going to be easy.

Even though I had a losing record my junior year, I had shown Coach Green how important the sport and the team were to me. The least I could do in return was show a commitment to becoming a better wrestler. I had continued to practice last season even after I was eliminated from the postseason. I had helped Coach Green out with his youth wrestling camp at Huntingtown over the summer, and had participated in one at the school, too. During the spring and summer, I had made it a routine to visit the weight room in order to put on enough muscle to eliminate the weight advantage my opponents originally held over me. I was getting pretty strong. When I started wrestling, I was able to bench press 120 pounds. The following summer, I was up to 160. By the start of practice my senior year, I was putting up 180 pounds, even though I weighed only 106. I was proud of how strong I had become, but all it took was Phil coming home over Thanksgiving to put me in my place. He teased me that he could squat 500 pounds, and asked how much I could squat. We both laughed at that.

I went up to Coach Green after practice to thank him for the honor.

"You earned it," he said. "Now don't screw it up."

I could forget about the captaincy being a reward. Coach Green's comment showed it was more of a responsibility, and that was a new feeling for me. Rarely had I been given much responsibility in my life. The only time I could remember such an instance was when my parents gave me our house keys when I started my freshman year at Central. Responsibility on this level was one of those things I had never experienced, so I didn't know I was missing out on something.

I felt so much more in command of myself throughout pre-season practice. I understood the sport, and it made such a difference in how much I enjoyed wrestling. While I had a blast during my junior season, I had more fun just being around teammates, and helping work toward a common goal. As a senior, I still felt that ambition, but I also knew what I was doing on the mat. I could appreciate the finer points of the sport. I could decipher between scoring a takedown through a series of strong tactical moves, rather than surprising my opponent—and myself—with a lucky thrust or slip. Strategy was a fun aspect to the sport that I did not discover until my senior season. It made me feel pretty confident in myself to be able to think two or three moves ahead of the situation. I saw that I didn't have to rely on strength to be successful.

I planned to exploit that advantage during my senior season. Among the 11 other schools in the Southern Maryland Athletic Conference, only three had their 103-pounders returning at that weight. That was consistent with the rest of the state; of the 16 103-pounders who qualified for the state tournament at the end of the 2004-05 season, only two returned at that weight for the 2005-06 season. The rest of them all grew over the summer and were now wrestling at higher weights. In their place came a lot of freshmen and sophomores. Rarely did upperclassmen—especially seniors—wrestle at 103 pounds. Most kids have grown too tall to be able to maintain a 103-pound body by the time they are 16- or 17-year-olds.

My new opponents had never wrestled anyone like me before. While I had that same advantage at the start of my junior season, I didn't know how to capitalize on it because I didn't know how to wrestle yet. I might have had them confused and a little bit scared, but I wasn't aggressive enough with them. Now they were confused, but they were scared for a different reason. They had all heard about me. They knew I was a team captain. They knew that team captains weren't slouches. No longer did they say, "Hey, what's up with the kid with no legs?" Instead, it was, "Wow, the kid with no legs is strong—and really good."

All that was left for me to do was prove it. I won my first match of the season in a meet with Bowie High School from Prince George's County. Then we headed to our first tournament at Kent County High on Maryland's Eastern Shore. The Maryland Public Secondary Schools Athletic Association limited member teams to three tournaments each regular season, in addition to their conference meets. I saw every tournament as a new opportunity to make a name for myself in the wrestling circles. Tournaments did wonders for my reputation. People had never heard about me when I went to our first tournament my junior year at Lackey High. From there, people spread the word about me throughout the Washington, D.C., area. When it came time for our second tournament two weeks later at Northern High, there was a buzz about me, and that drew several hundred people to the meet.

There was plenty of intrigue about me at the start of my senior year. By that time, people knew that I wasn't a gimmick. I did very well for a first-year wrestler, and many observers wondered where I would go from there. Of course, there was plenty of skepticism, too. Some fans thought there was a limit to how much I, or any wrestler, for that matter, could learn in such a short amount of time. There was no substitute for experience, and that was often a decisive factor in this sport. My critics thought that, eventually, my opponents—especially the ones who had been wrestling for several years—would figure me out, and I wouldn't have that psychological edge over my opponents. There was a lot on the line for me in our first tournament of my senior year: I had to start the season on a positive note and prove that Coach's commitment to me was warranted.

Kent County High was close to two hours from Huntingtown, and we stayed overnight in a hotel there for the two days of the tournament. There were nine other teams at the tournament, but only two from the Washington, D.C., area—a couple of schools from the northern edge, closer to Baltimore. That provided me with another chance to prove myself to a whole new group of wrestlers who had never seen me before.

I won my two matches on Friday night, and then one more Saturday morning to advance to the 103-pound final. It was my first championship match, and it took some getting used to. After I won the semifinal match around noon, I had a long wait for the final. The consolation rounds took place all afternoon, and the championship matches for each weight class were all held together in the evening. I never had to wait like that at tournaments my junior year. I was always wrestling through the consolation brackets, and those matches usually came up every two or three hours. I finished sixth, fifth, and fourth in my three tournaments that year, so I never had to worry about killing time. By the time I had cooled down after a match, it was time to start psyching myself up for my next match.

I didn't know what to do with my time at Kent. It was seven hours between matches. I didn't know anyone from the other teams in the tournament, and Curk was my only teammate to qualify for a final. I sat in the bleachers for a while and saw a couple of my teammates begin to get ready for their consolation matches. I thought about being in their situation last year. I was upset that I had lost. While it was nice to keep wrestling and try for third place, it still was disappointing to be eliminated from championship contention. I figured those guys felt the same way, so I decided to give them as much support as I could. I was, after all, a captain. That was a job of the captain.

I went to each teammate's match and sat along the side of the mat or just in front of the bleachers. I don't know if that helped them at all, but I know that whenever I wrestled and I could see Phil watching my match, it made me feel good. It also challenged me. I had to put on a good show in front of the captain. As I watched our 140-pounder, Ryan Corken, get ready for his third-place match, it suddenly hit me—I was wrestling for first place. This was a chance for me to be at the top of the medal stand when the tournament officials award the top six finishers in each weight class at the end of the tournament.

Wrestling tournaments know how to add drama to the championship round. There was only one mat in the center of the gymnasium, and the lights were turned off for the introduction of the finalists. Some tournaments shined a spotlight on the middle of the mat. One finalist from each weight class lined up on one side of the mat, while his opponent lined up on the opposite side. The public address announcer would call out our names and schools, and we came to the center of the mat to shake hands before returning to the line. I had never experienced such a thrill in my short time in wrestling.

As my match approached, my stomach felt like it was tied in knots. I wasn't the kind of person who got nervous, but I had never been in a situation where this many people were watching—and judging—me. What if I got my butt kicked in front of them?

I didn't. I lost, 4-2, to a kid I had never seen—and never saw again—from tiny Stephen Decatur High in western Maryland. Just like with every loss, I was disappointed with myself. I didn't take the time to look back on the significance of how far I had advanced. As I sat in the bleachers with my teammates waiting for Curk's match, I discussed a couple of sequences and showed where I could have scored points, or avoided getting taken down and giving up points. This was something I couldn't do my junior year; I couldn't critique my wrestling this carefully, and if I could, I needed to watch the video of the match first. But I had learned to memorize critical moments, so I could try to repeat the successful ones and avoid those that doomed me.

Katie DeVore was there to watch her brother, Sean. She sat beside me after my match, and tired of my complaining.

"Stop it already," she said. "You *are* doing better. You finished second in your first tournament this year. You were sixth in your first tournament last year."

I hated to admit it, but she was right. I was a finalist in a competitive tournament, and that gave me the confidence that I could contend at a high level. That was a winnable match for me. I didn't get my butt kicked. I had a chance to win until the final buzzer, and there was no way I could have said that eight months earlier at the end of my junior season.

The difference in those eight months came from three areas. My improved strength was one. I couldn't be pushed around anymore. I had made up that weight difference, and now I was a 103-pounder wrestling other 103-pounders. I also improved my knowledge of the sport. I knew I could depend upon certain moves to score points. These were moves that benefited me, in particular. I couldn't watch other wrestlers and copy their tactics. I needed to focus on moves that took advantage of my strength: being low to the ground.

With a single-leg takedown, for example, I would use both my arms to grab my opponent's upper thigh—which was eye level for me—and use my torso to force his body to the mat. I could almost always count on getting two points every time I tried that move. My opponent's only alternative to defend that move was to crouch down to guard his legs, and that compromised his ability to attack me.

Lastly, I was more mature. I had learned to put myself in a wrestling frame of mind long before the opening whistle. It was so much fun to have a group of teammates by my side all the time—be it at practice, on the bus to meets, or in the bleachers before a match. During my junior season, I enjoyed taking advantage of that time together with those guys. I ultimately discovered, however, that I needed to be better prepared mentally before each match. And that couldn't start five minutes before I got onto the mat. My teammates would joke with me every so often about the way I went off on my own to warm up. I liked to bounce around on my hands and sway the upper part of my body back and forth, almost as if I was making a circular outline against the air. I got into a pretty good rhythm with my body, and once I was in that rhythm, it was hard to catch my attention. I would stretch out my back and neck by trying to make a circle with my head and the bottom of my torso. Of course, I didn't come close, but I'm sure it freaked out a few opponents or other wrestlers who saw that, and couldn't come close to contorting their bodies the way I could. I looked so determined and focused when I warmed up that my teammate Michael Groves, our senior 130-pounder, said I seemed to have the attitude of a pit bull packed into the body of a Chihuahua.

The pit bull stayed home, though, when we went to our next tournament at Northern High School the week after New Year's. In between, I had rolled up four more victories at regular meets, and on the basis of my 8-1 record, I was the top-seeded 103-pounder at the tournament. I came in confident, remembering how that tournament was the place where a large part of the wrestling community first had its chance to see me the year before. I knew it was hard to be sentimental after doing something for just over a year, but coming to the Northern Tournament brought back fond memories.

Unfortunately, the lasting memories I will have of that event happened my senior year. It was probably the worst weekend of my career, and definitely the most disappointing. After I won my first match, I faced Jake Shilling, a sophomore from La Plata High School and someone I was quite familiar with from competing in the Southern Maryland Athletic Conference. Shilling had beaten me twice my junior season, and I was looking forward to getting revenge. But revenge would have to wait for another day.

Shilling had the right idea about how to wrestle me. It was tough for opponents to score points on takedowns against me because I had such little body to grab on to. It wasn't like guys could go for my legs, and try to take me down that way. I had learned to protect myself from being put on my back, so I always leaned forward. If anyone came at me, I shot the bottom part of my torso out from under me, and landed on my stomach, while

I grabbed at my opponent's leg. Wrestlers can only secure a pin when their opponent is on his back, so this moved worked in my favor.

It was possible, though, for my opponents to score points without gaining control of my body. For example, anytime a wrestler breaks free from an opponent's control, he is awarded one point. It could come right off the whistle, or it could come from a long clench. Sometimes, the escape is the one point a wrestler needs to win, whether it is a back-and-forth match, or a slow-paced one, where one or both wrestlers are hesitant to make moves.

At the Northern Tournament, Shilling beat me using a smart strategy, and I was furious. He had begun to figure me out. He knew how tough it was to score a takedown on me, so he scored his escape points and tried to make those hold up. He would get me on my stomach, hop onto my back and ride me until the referee called a stalemate or said Shilling was stalling. He would try to flip me over on my back, but always made sure he never relinquished control, which would let me score two points for reversing control.

I went home angry with myself that night and didn't return the next morning with a clear head. I paid for it in my second match, when I lost to a kid I had just beaten four days earlier in a team dual meet. I finished the tournament in fifth place, and I was livid. All the optimism I had generated for both my teammates and myself in the weeks leading up to that tournament, I had promptly flushed away with how I wrestled that weekend. I took a couple of steps backward for the first time in my wrestling career.

Nobody had shown more faith in me nor given me more encouragement in the 15 months I had been wrestling than Coach Green. Whenever I felt down, I may not have shown it, but Coach Green could sense it, and he would try to lift my spirits and motivate me. It didn't take extensive knowledge of the sport to do this; he just read people so well and knew how to push their buttons.

The following Friday night we piled into the gymnasium at South River High School in Anne Arundel County. I placed fourth at that tournament during my junior year, which was my best finish of the season. Our team staked out a section of the bleachers and dropped our bags off before heading over to the scales for weigh-in. Eighteen teams were there for the tournament my senior year. We were joking around a bit before Coach Green came over with the tournament draw sheets in his hand. I was sitting midway up the bleachers, and he headed right toward me. All of my teammates were sitting near me when Coach Green showed me the 103-pound draw sheet. Despite my horrible finish at the Northern Tournament, my overall record still gave me the top seed in the tournament. I was stunned.

"You see that?" Coach Green said to me, as he pointed to my name at the top of the 103-pound bracket. "Don't screw it up."

Each one of my teammates heard his comment, but none of them said anything to me about it. This was strictly a conversation between Coach Green and me, and it spoke volumes. At this time last year, Coach was happy that I had stuck with wrestling and showed some improvement. I remember him telling a newspaper reporter after I finished fourth in that tournament as a junior that I was "on fire" that weekend. He was thrilled for me. But now, if I finished fourth again, I figured I would have to walk back to Huntingtown. This was the first time Coach Green explicitly stated he expected me to perform at a certain level. He knew how much I had improved, and his standards had risen. He wasn't asking me to do well. He was asking me to win, and I had never done that before at a tournament.

Some people might have considered this pressure. I just thought it was another responsibility of being captain. Coach Green saw how disappointed he and I both were in my performance the previous weekend. Every wrestler—every athlete—goes through an occasional slump and falls short of his or her potential. But the good ones are able to rebound and show it was just a fluke. Coach Green knew that each one of my teammates had a tournament like that once before. He wanted their captain to show them how to recover.

I don't know if I had ever been more motivated to perform as I was that weekend. I rolled through my first three matches Friday night and Saturday morning to secure a spot in the final later that evening. I got off the mat following my semifinal match and wondered what Coach Green thought about that. I thought I had answered his challenge pretty well.

"Trevon, get everyone out in the hallway," he told me. "Now!"

I never saw Coach Green angrier. As a team, we were wrestling horribly, and he let us know. I was the only one from our team to advance to a final, and six of the 10 other wrestlers we brought to the tournament were eliminated from placing in the top six of their class. That was completely unacceptable for Coach Green. Even the four guys who did place each lost their last matches, and finished sixth instead of fifth, or fourth instead of third.

Coach Green told me I could go home and relax during the afternoon, before my final, but I couldn't take him up on his offer. My teammates were at their weakest point and they needed me there. Curk Smart told me to take a nap in the bleachers so I would be fully charged for the final. But I couldn't even do that. My stepfather suggested I at least lie down and rest. Every time I did, though, another one of my teammates was wrestling in a consolation-round match, and I needed to be at the mat to root him on.

The day wore on, and Huntingtown's bad results poured in. As it came closer to the finals, my stomach started to hurt again. At the Kent Tournament, at least I had Curk there with me wrestling in his final. I had nobody else at South River to share the burden. It was all on me. I could prevent the weekend from being a complete washout for Huntingtown if I could take first place. And if I lost? I didn't want to imagine the bus ride home or Monday's practice. There was never a more perfect—or necessary—moment for me to win my first tournament. As I warmed up just prior to my match, I told myself over and over, "It's got to be here. It's got to be here."

My opponent was Chas Guy from Chopticon High School, another team in the Southern Maryland Athletic Conference. I had defeated him, 4-2, in my junior year in a dual meet, but I knew that result meant little a year later. Not only had we both improved, but the stakes were much higher at South River. Following the introductions, I took off my warm-ups, all the while repeating in my head, "It's got to be here." My stomach was still in knots, and it felt like something was poking at me from inside. Nothing I tried relieved the pain.

Once the match began, I couldn't think about my stomach. Instead, I was focused on Guy's wrists. He was leaning over to guard from me attacking his legs. For the first minute, I chased him around the mat. My plan was to grab his wrist and yank him down. With about 30 seconds left in the first period, I was able to get underneath his right knee, and I had a firm grasp of his leg. He tried to hop away to break free from me, but he couldn't get away. Seven seconds before the end of the period, I flipped him over and scored a two-point takedown.

After an uneventful second period, we began a third period I would never forget—for the wrong reason. Midway through the period, I had control of him, but the score was only 2-0 in my favor, and a takedown or reversal for him would tie things up. Then, all of a sudden, I saw his left hand stretch across my torso from the top to the bottom and reach right for my crotch. With his fingers spread, he grabbed me. I screamed. In a couple of my previous matches, I had been kicked in the crotch, but that was accidental. I had also seen instances when a wrestler would grab an opponent's arm and pull it between his opponent's legs toward the back, and his crotch would get in the way. Everyone reacted differently. Some of them crouched down in pain. Others charged after their opponent, only to have the referee step in between. Each time I saw it happen, though, I winced in pain and told whoever was next to me, "Let that never happen to me."

Never, though, had I seen—let alone experienced—a case where someone did this on purpose. Opponents had head-butted me before, because they tried to take me down by charging into me. In fact, it happened in my semifinal match earlier in the day, and it opened up about a pea-sized cut underneath my right eye. It drew blood and I was wearing a small bandage as a result. A grab between my legs, though, was the absolute last thing on my mind. I never went into a match thinking I had to guard against a move like that. It caught me by surprise and it made me mad. I was losing focus, and my mind wasn't on the title anymore. Even though I was awarded two penalty points, I was vulnerable. The match wasn't over yet, and it didn't take long to lose a match. My emotions could overtake me, and I could do something really stupid. Just the previous weekend at the Northern Tournament, I saw a fellow wrestler with a comfortable 8-2 lead with 30 seconds left in the third period get pinned as the clock wound down.

I kept my emotions in check well enough to hold on to win the match, 4-0. I knew everyone was watching me, so I couldn't do anything stupid after the match. We shook hands at the center of the mat, and the referee raised my hand. I went to shake the opposing coach's hand, and raced off the mat. I didn't even go back to Coach Green. I needed to rest. I stood underneath the bleachers and regained my composure. I took one deep breath after another. About a minute later, three of my teammates found me.

"Dude, you won," Curk yelled out. "Congratulations!"

In that moment, my anger disappeared and a smile snuck onto my face. I had won a tournament. I was a champion. Coach Green came by, sporting a big smile, a startling change from just a few hours earlier. After the 112-pound final, there was a medal ceremony for the 103-pound class. It meant so much to climb onto that medal stand at the very top. The medal stand is arranged such that the champion's spot is about three feet off of the ground, allowing him to stand taller than his competitors. Coach Green joked with me afterward that, even with the higher stand, I still stood shorter than the other five place-winners.

"Nice job, sixth place," he said with a laugh.

My teammates laughed, too, but none of them had a bigger smile than I did. This was hard proof of an accomplishment that the majority of high school wrestlers never achieve. Even for just one day, I could call myself the best.

Even though I had improved dramatically as a wrestler, I wasn't receiving the same media attention during my senior year that

I had during my junior year. I had no problem with that. It allowed me to stay focused and concentrate on my wrestling and schoolwork. But I got an occasional interruption, including one that I never expected.

Kevin James was a magician who was part of a nightly show at a Las Vegas hotel. He had read about me in newspaper articles and visited me at school in January 2006. He came with a business proposition: as long as I was a part of his magic show, he would pay every penny of my college expenses. I was intrigued, of course, and told him my parents and I would meet with him. We had no idea what he wanted me to do in his magic show, but his offer was just too tempting to ignore—especially for a family like mine.

He arrived to meet me just moments before we had a home match against Lackey High. My parents were there with me, and he explained his deal. There was a part of his magic show where he would saw a man in half. Then, with the audience shocked, he would show the man returned to his original self. He wanted me to be that man. I would wear my prosthesis in order to make the scam work. It was a few minutes before the start of the match, and I needed to get ready. I asked if we could talk after the match, which he agreed to do.

"Can you get up and walk around?" he asked. "I want to see what you can do. This will only take a minute."

I was in a very difficult position. Poor black families didn't have people walk into their lives from out of nowhere and give them a lot of money. Sure enough, that's what James wanted to do. It was a college education—potentially worth a couple hundred thousand dollars—all for the taking. All I had to do was a little work. But it was demeaning work. James saw a way to fool people by making a joke of my body. How much was my self-esteem worth? I had to determine whether it was a fair trade for a once-in-a-lifetime opportunity.

Before I could, though, my stepfather decided it for us.

"Let me ask you this," he said to James. "If he had legs, would you be here?"

"Well, no," James replied.

"That's what I thought. I don't want you turning him into a freak show."

My stepfather walked away, and James left Huntingtown. I would have to wait for another once-in-a-lifetime opportunity, but in the meantime, I kept something more valuable—my dignity.

The wrestling postseason began on February 17 with the two-day Southern Maryland Athletic Conference tournament. The site changed each year; my junior year, we hosted it at Huntingtown, but this year, it was at Chopticon High, about 40 miles away.

We all had a good idea of what was going to happen as far as I was concerned: Jake Shilling and I were clearly the top two 103-pounders in the conference, and the preliminary rounds were just a formality until we met for a third time. He had beaten me just two weeks earlier in our final dual meet of the regular season.

We both easily advanced to Saturday night's final. By reaching the final, I had qualified for the following week's 3A South Regional tournament, the last step before the state tournament. Even though I knew I had at least one more weekend of wrestling left in my career, I thought about how it was starting to come to an end. The bad part about the postseason was that I never knew which match would be my last. Any given match could be my last time on the mat. It wasn't just the time on the mat that I enjoyed, but also the scene at tournaments. There were so many friendly faces I had met over the course of those two wrestling seasons. They were staples at many of the meets and tournaments I attended, and I spent the Saturday afternoon at Chopticon talking to many of those people.

And many of those people sought me out, too. I loved the attention. Even if my teammates weren't wrestling in the consolation rounds, I couldn't tune out the people inside that gymnasium. I spent a good part of that afternoon talking to people, while waiting for that evening's final match with Shilling. Of course, I loved the interest from the girls at those tournaments, but my senior year brought out a new group of fans—other wrestlers. By that time I was wrestling for a SMAC championship, so instead of asking me about what it was like to wrestle with no legs, they were asking me for tips on the mat.

There were rows of bleachers on three sides of the gymnasium at Chopticon, and by the time the championship round began, they were all just about full. Wrestling is a big sport, not just in Calvert County, but also all over the tri-county region of

Southern Maryland. The sport suits the majority of its residents—blue-collar and working-class. I wasn't living up to that label all afternoon. Rather than psyching myself up, and tweaking a game plan that might finally work against Shilling, I horsed around with friends and tried to sweet-talk some girls. I paid for my laziness, because I let Shilling do exactly what he did the previous four times we had faced each other. While he waited for his chance to score a point, Shilling kept me on my stomach and let the clock tick away. He rode my back for the last half-minute of the second period, as he sandwiched my torso with his legs, which he locked together at his ankles. I hated him for it, but it was a smart move.

With still no score, the third period began with me in the offensive starting position. I had to act quickly because Shilling was on his knees, and if he escaped right off the draw, that would probably give him the one point he needed for the victory, given how the first two periods had progressed. Shilling scored that escape right off the opening whistle, but then the biggest surprise of the match occurred. I grabbed his right thigh and scored a two-point takedown just 10 seconds after his escape. I was ahead 2-1, and still had his leg cradled in my arms. From his seat at the edge of the mat, I heard Coach Green yelling, "Keep the leg, keep the leg." With 47 seconds left, there was a whistle for a stalemate. Right after wrestling resumed, Shilling scored a reversal to go back ahead, 3-2, with just 40 seconds left.

I didn't give up. With 10 seconds to go, I had him on his side. All I needed to do was turn him over, and I would have had a two-point reversal and a victory. I tried to bury my shoulder into his chest to force him over, but the final horn sounded, and I had to settle for second place. I stormed off the mat and headed to the corner of the gymnasium. I knew I had blown that match, and I wasn't going to forgive myself for it.

Fortunately, I had another chance at Shilling—the following week at the 3A South Region tournament at Westlake High School in Charles County, not too far from La Plata. The top four finishers earned spots in the field of 16 at the state tournament. Shilling and I were the top two seeds, and we breezed through the opening rounds to the final again. Even though my semifinal victory clinched a spot for me in the state tournament, I wasn't thinking about that. Shilling had beaten me five straight times. None of that would matter, though, if I beat him in the regional final.

I thought about where I had failed in our previous match and tried to focus on correcting my mistakes. I made sure that during my break before the championship match, I had the time and the environment needed to concentrate. I kept a straight face all afternoon, which was so unusual for me that several people asked me if I was okay.

"I'm just getting ready for tonight," I told each of them.

Shilling always liked to lean down and in toward me and keep his legs out of my arms' reach. I started the first period by going high on him and tried to bring him to the mat by grabbing on to his head. Thirty seconds into the match, though, I found my opening and snatched his left thigh. Shilling always had excellent balance, which was how he could wrestle me effectively even though he leaned down with his upper body. He was showing that again when I had my arms wrapped around his left thigh. For 30 seconds, he stayed upright. I kept twisting my body, hoping that one jerk of his leg would drop him.

Finally, at the midway point of the period, he fell down, landing on his left side. Coach Green yelled out, "Two, two, two!" to tell the referee to raise his right hand and credit me with a two-point takedown. But the referee wasn't budging. There were several instances during the season when I didn't get credit for points because some referees still weren't sure how to judge my matches. They look for a wrestler to have total control of his opponent's body before awarding points. One of the easiest ways to determine that is by seeing if a wrestler's legs are wrapped around his opponent's hips. In that case, the opponent is usually helpless. He can't move his lower body. I couldn't make a move like that. When I had my opponent on the ground, I could only control half of my opponent's body at a time, and I always chose his upper half.

That was the case here, and I received no points for my hard work. The referee called a stalemate with 24 seconds left in the first period, and I had to relinquish my hold. The second period began again with Shilling protecting his legs very well. I chased him around the mat for much of the period until a stalemate was called with 22 seconds left. Off the starting position, Shilling broke free and scored the match's first point with an escape. I was worried because he had his point and was going to protect it for the rest of the match. I knew my opportunities would be limited.

I began the third period in the defensive starting position. If I could escape, it would tie the match. Shilling knew this and wouldn't let me. He forced me onto my stomach, climbed onto my back and made sure he didn't move. He wrapped his arms underneath my chest and locked his hands. Other opponents had done this before, and it was easy to use it to disguise stalling. I was very difficult to flip over because I had such long arms, which I spread out on the mat when I was on my stomach. Most opponents could not reach my hands to pull them off the ground. They weren't going to get off of my back, because that would give me an easy opportunity to escape. As a result, some opponents were able to stay on my back for 30 or 45 seconds without a stalemate or stall called. Referees couldn't tell whether they were struggling or stalling.

When the final horn sounded, I was still on my stomach. I buried my face into the mat for a couple of seconds, before I got up, shook Shilling's hand, and watched the referee raise it in victory. I was devastated. It didn't matter that I was going on to the state tournament, an honor that labeled me one of the best wrestlers in Maryland. Throughout my two seasons of wrestling, I had trained and learned to improve my skills, and, ultimately, get better results. Yet, this was one opponent for whom I had prepared more thoroughly than any other, and I still couldn't beat him.

I went to sleep angry that night, oblivious to the fact that six days later, I would be wrestling on the biggest stage in the state.

I arrived at school on Monday morning, and my teammate
Curk Smart saw me in the hallway in between classes.

"Did you see the draw?" he asked me.

The state tournament draw had been released, and it was
done very systematically. The four regional champions were the
top seeds, and each faced a different region's fourth-place finish-
er in the first round. The second- and third-place wrestlers in the
regions were paired off in their pockets of the bracket. The top
two wrestlers in each region were placed on separate sides of the
bracket, so they could not meet until the championship. It bothered me that it was going to take a situation like that for me to
get another shot at Jake Shilling. Of course, there was a chance
we could meet in the consolation rounds, but a match there
wouldn't have the same drama. We would have both lost by that
time and been reduced to fighting for third place.

But I took one look at the draw, and that was all it took to wipe Shilling from my mind. My first-round match was against a kid I had never heard of, from a town north of Baltimore. If I won that match, though, I probably would face the top seed—Will Sharbaugh, the only remaining undefeated 103-pounder in the state. I knew the draw was predetermined, but this didn't make me feel any better. I was 26-6, and only two other wrestlers—Shilling, whose record was 32-5, and Jeremy Seipp, who went 31-3 for North Carroll High School—had fewer losses than I did. Coach Green told us at practice later that day that rankings meant nothing. I needed to hear that, because I had just about given myself a second-round loss.

For the first time in my wrestling career, I had a tough week sleeping. The whole idea of competing in the state tournament was tough to settle in my mind. I had thought about this since the middle of my junior year, when it became apparent that I could succeed in the sport. After going to watch Phil Riley win his championship the previous year, I dreamed of wrestling on one of those eight mats on the floor of Cole Field House. I wasn't thinking of being on the medal stand, but rather, winning one match after another, and hearing people cheer after each one, much like our team did for Phil. The satisfaction of working harder than I ever had in my career and benefiting from that effort was what drove me more than anything else that week.

The first three days of that week, I practiced alongside wrestlers from a few of the Southern Maryland schools who were going to the state tournament. Those were the three hardest practices of my life, more difficult than even that first practice my junior year when I trudged through the hallways on my hands. Calvert High Coach Dave Kistler structured his practices differently than Coach Green did. Instead of going at one opponent for 10 or 15 minutes, Kistler rotated four or five different guys against one another for one minute apiece. It taught me to adapt to a different opponent almost instantaneously, and it wore me out.

At the end of Wednesday's practice, the last one we all had together, Kistler gathered us together and said, "You're each among the top 16 in the state. Think about that. No matter what you do from here on, nobody can take that away from you." Then, he went on to say how he wouldn't be surprised if we each finished as place-winners, the top six in our weight classes.

This was nothing I hadn't heard before. When Coach Green and I casually discussed my goals, they changed around midseason from just qualifying for the state tournament to placing at the state tournament. Coach Green always believed in my abilities, but it was so important to hear another person tell me this.

As we boarded the bus to go home from Westlake after the regional tournament, one of our team managers told me she couldn't make it to the state tournament.

"This is the last time I'm going to see you wrestle," she said.

The end of wrestling really crept up on me with her comment, and I hadn't thought about it. It was the last week of

February, and a few friends and I had already started counting down the final days of school, to which we all looked forward. I hadn't thought about the end of wrestling, though.

I remembered about the all the good times I had with wrestling, both on and off the mat. There was going to be a last time for everything. On our way home that night, I thought, "This is my last bus ride." I always considered the bus rides to be therapeutic. No matter what happened, whether I won or lost my match that night, or whether the entire team or just me and a couple other guys were on the bus, I always rode it home. The bus ride home allowed me time to replay the match in my head. It allowed me to think about what I did right and what I regretted. Once I got off the bus, I was able to separate myself from wrestling.

But I couldn't detach myself from my teammates, and I thought about that at Thursday's practice, the day before the start of the state tournament. It was my last practice, the last time I would come into the wrestling room during my free final period to mop and sanitize the mats. It was the last time I could hang out in that room with my teammates, who helped me create such a memorable two years at the school. These were the guys who challenged me to become better—both as a wrestler and a person. Collectively, they were as responsible as anyone for me qualifying for the state tournament. There are certain memories I have that can never be duplicated, because I made them with these teammates. I could grab four close friends, and we could take a scrawny freshman and tape him to the roll used to bind up the wrestling mat. We could all laugh loudly as the naïve freshman playfully tried to break free.

But it would never be as funny or unforgettable as it was when my senior teammates Sean DeVore, A.J. Gerdes, Michael Groves, and Curk Smart joined me in doing that to freshman Markus Jarboe, my practice partner during my senior year. Anyone could have walked into that room and had no idea Curk, A.J., and I were less than 24 hours from the start of the state tournament.

Along with five of my teammates, Coach Green and I arrived at the Cole Field House on the University of Maryland campus around noon on March 3, 2006. It was bitterly cold outside, and once we entered the building we were stuck in a vestibule with six doors that led into the main arena. None of them would open. "Let me try this," I said, as I approached the button that opens the door electronically for handicapped people. Sure enough, a door opened. It was the first sign that a disabled person could feel right at home at the state wrestling tournament.

I thought I knew what to expect when we entered Cole. After all, I had seen the eight mats laid out across the floor of the 14,500-seat arena when I came in support of my teammate Phil Riley the previous year. It was a different perspective, though, being on the floor and looking up at all the people in the stands. I looked around and saw wrestlers warming up beside me; the year before, when I sat in the stands, they appeared far off in the distance.

"I wrestled for four years," my stepfather told me. "I know the meaning of getting here. This is where you want to be."

I was new to the majority of the field. Of the 15 other 103-pounders, I had wrestled only four of them—and a fifth was at the South River tournament and had a chance to see me in action. I hoped I could take advantage of my opponents' unfamiliarity with me. I also had an edge in maturity; I was the only senior among the 16 entrants. Four were freshmen, there were nine sophomores and two juniors. I wasn't just new to my opponents; the public address announcer mispronounced my first name when I was introduced for my first match. It was just what I needed to lighten the mood.

My opponents not only had to devise a strategy for defeating me, they also had to feel comfortable with me. Nick Damron once told me that he felt out of place the first time he faced me because he was trained to go after his opponent's legs. When he saw me for the first time, he had to ditch half of his game plan. He also told me how awkward he felt about grabbing the lower part of my body, and that was something I expected from most teenagers, whether or not they were wrestling me. They didn't know where my body ended, nor did they know if the body parts I had were anatomically correct. Many opponents were afraid to put their hands anywhere on my body lower than my chest.

My first opponent at the state tournament was exactly that way. He looked so apprehensive about touching me, kind of like my teammates were when I first started coming to open mats and they thought I was fragile. I wasted no time taking advantage of that uneasiness to score a takedown just 17 seconds into the match. At the start of the second period, I was in defensive starting position, and my opponent was trying to turn me over. He kept grasping at my hips because that's what he did against opponents who had legs. Twenty seconds later, I scored a two-point reversal to go up 4-0. Even though I gave him an escape point, I scored another reversal with 40 seconds left and finished the second period ahead, 6-1. It was more of the same in the third period. He was afraid to go low on me, and I kept powering away on him. The final horn sounded and I won, 8-3. I was relieved. I got through my first state tournament match just fine.

Three mats over from where I wrestled, Will Sharbaugh pinned his first-round opponent in 34 seconds to run his season record to 34-0. I had a little over three hours to prepare for him. As I found the stairs leading from the floor to the seats, I spotted Mr. Gray walking down the aisle. I hadn't seen him in more than a year, and my eyes bulged out like saucers. He had seen me at a tournament and a meet during my junior year, but I was so much improved since then. It meant the world to me that my first true mentor, the person who first challenged me athletically, was there to watch me at my crowning athletic moment.

I went back to the section of the stands where our team and friends were spread out. Everyone offered me congratulations and well wishes, but it was difficult to pay attention to them. The biggest match of my life was in front of me. I knew I wasn't an unknown anymore. The whole state had either seen or at least heard about me. Not once during the tournament did any of my teammates or I hear, "Hey, did you hear about the kid here with no legs?" Just as I had done several times prior in my life, I had managed to fit in. I had been accepted by the state-wide wrestling community, but now it was time to prove that I belonged at the elite level. Even though I had advanced to the state tournament, I thought many people didn't consider me a legitimate wrestler, just someone who had an inspiring story and smiled when he was spoken to. I knew that could all change with one match.

Sharbaugh was about an inch or two taller than most of my opponents, and I figured that could only benefit me. It meant he had a higher center of gravity and needed to crouch down further in order to guard against me shooting at his legs. I was hoping for any advantage possible as introductions were made prior to the start of the match.

The referee blew the opening whistle, and Sharbaugh immediately showed me why he was the best wrestler in the state. In my 68 previous high school matches over two years, no opponent did what Sharbaugh did right away: He charged at me. Every other opponent always took a step backward. When I was quick enough, I caught them, and scored a fast takedown. What they never realized was how vulnerable I was to someone charging at me with all their momentum. I had neither the strength nor the balance to stay upright under an attack like that. Anyone who got me on my back knew I was a dead man—just like I had been in my first high school match as a junior.

But Sharbaugh didn't get me on my back. I was able to slide to the side, and keep him at arm's length. But 20 seconds into the match, he was able to flip me over and score a takedown. I escaped five seconds later to cut his lead to 2-1. I began the second period in defensive starting position. Sharbaugh was behind me and he was not going to let me break free. He had me down on my stomach, wrapped his arms around my chest, and locked his hands together right over my heart. There was only one stalemate called—midway through the period.

He began the third period down on his stomach, but escaped 45 seconds into the period to go up 3-1. Now, I needed a takedown if I was to have a chance. Sharbaugh, though, was so good at keeping me at bay. He was so quick, that every time I shot in, he kicked his feet out backward, and collapsed forward on top of me. We were on the edge of the circle and I tried to pull him out of bounds so we could start back in the middle. With four seconds left, he took me down, just before his feet left the circle and he fell out of bounds. He was up 5-1. The escape he gave me off the draw happened just before the final buzzer. I lost, 5-2.

I shook hands and then dashed off the mat. I didn't even notice the standing ovation from the spectators sitting in the sections near our mat. As I left the mat, I threw my body against the cushioned wall behind the scorer's table. I clenched my teeth, and took several deep breaths. I needed all the help I could get at that moment to fight off the tears welling up in my eyes.

Just like I had been with my last loss to Shilling, I was hurt less by the fact that I lost, and more by the closeness of it. This one hurt even more because of how close I was to beating the best wrestler in the state. Sharbaugh went on to win the state championship. In fact, he won his last two matches very convincingly, 6-0, and, 12-5. He told reporters afterward that my match was his toughest of the tournament.

Coaches and event officials stopped as they walked along the arena floor to tell Coach Green and I how much I had impressed them. They didn't say it, but each of them had that same tone—a puzzled amazement—in their voices that my classmates had when they first learned I wrestled. These men were hardcore wrestling followers, and even they wondered how someone with no legs took the best wrestler in the state to the limit. Their congratulations were sincere, and not those hollow "keep-it-ups" I had heard throughout my childhood. To the few remaining skeptics, I proved to them I was a legitimate wrestler.

But there was no more legitimate wrestling for me that night. I had to come back the next morning, with dreams of third place. It didn't sound right.

In the moments before the first matches of the state tournament began on Friday—just prior to my first-round victory—the air was thick with anticipation. Every wrestler in the building was thinking, "Why not me?" It was an interesting mix of optimism, excitement, and tension. But by the time I was stretching on the mats at 9 a.m. Saturday, that feeling was gone. It was like everyone was still asleep, even the people there. The championship rounds didn't resume until two hours later, so many of the state-title hopefuls hadn't arrived yet. In fact, the arena was pretty empty compared to the previous evening. I could hear a couple of kids from Northern's team section yell out, "Go Trevon."

I was stretching out to prepare for the first round of the consolation tournament. Everyone who didn't advance to a final dropped into this bracket. Later on in the day, the semifinal losers would also drop into this tournament, and they could fall to as far as sixth place. Coach Green demanded that I maintain a good attitude. "Forget about last night," he told me. He knew I was steamed about that loss, but I couldn't dwell on it. Here, he said, was my chance to do something that nobody would have predicted—finish third in the state as a second-year wrestler. There was no mention of "not having legs."

I went after my first opponent like I did the day before—aggressively and fearlessly. He didn't stand a chance. I scored a takedown 25 seconds in, was ahead 5-0 by the end of the second period, and finished with the easiest 9-1 victory a state-tournament qualifier could envision. Three hours later, in the consolation quarterfinals, I faced another wrestler who I intimidated very easily. I scored on a reversal about a half-minute into the match, and he stayed away from me until the third period, when I started in the defensive position. Between an escape, a couple of takedowns, and a reversal in the next 90 seconds, I had another easy victory, 9-2.

I had just over an hour to get ready for my next match, but that wasn't a worry. When the match began, I knew I was in good shape. My opponent spent more time looking at his coaches during our match than at me. He didn't know what to do. He draped his arms around me in the hope that I would go down in a way that could score him points. Midway through the second period, we rolled out of bounds, and as we returned to the middle, my opponent's coaches tried to give him the "How-to-wrestle-Trevon-Jenifer" lesson in 10 seconds. It didn't work. I won 3-1.

It was my 30th victory of the season, and I was impressed that I had hit that milestone. All day, I began every match knowing that it could be the last of my high school career. After I won my consolation semifinal, there was only one match left: a competition for third place. Whether I won or lost, that would be the end of my high school wrestling career.

I had spent the past week thinking about each "last" of wrestling—the last bus ride, the last practice, and the last weigh-in. Never, though, did I think about what my last match would be like. Part of me didn't want to confront that reality, even though it was inevitable. Also, though, I didn't want to put so much pressure on myself to feel like I had to wrestle the perfect match. My career was already a fairy tale. One match couldn't change the storyline.

So I treated the match the way I wanted it to treat me—normally. I wasn't going to prepare for it any differently. I found my teammates sitting in the stands and enjoyed the last moments of hanging out as part of the Huntingtown wrestling team. We didn't discuss the end of my career. Instead, we talked about things going on at school. I told Mike and Curk that I wouldn't even get any time off to recuperate from a tiring wrestling season; softball practice had begun three days before, and I had plans to be a manager again. Monday afternoon would be my first practice of the season.

About a half-hour before my match, Coach Green and I headed for the tunnel that led out to the arena floor. I went through my typical stretches and kept to myself, while Coach Green talked to other coaches who were there with their wrestlers warming up for their third-place matches. I didn't realize it, but I warmed up underneath a sign hanging over the tunnel that read, "Maryland State Wrestling Tournament." A snapshot of that image would have been an appropriate advertisement for the event. From all the attention I was receiving from people I had never met, I knew I was the story of the event—a very humbling feeling.

I began my third-place match with the same aggressiveness that had become my trademark. I grabbed my opponent's left thigh right away and scored a two-point takedown 20 seconds into first period. He didn't have much of a chance. I was in total control the entire match, especially after my two-point reversal in the opening seconds of the second period made the score 4-0. The only point he gained was an escape two seconds before the end of the third period.

The fifth-place match was happening on the adjacent mat, and on the other side of the arena floor were the third- and fifth-place matches in the small schools tournament. But I had the crowd's full attention. There was applause from people all around the arena as the referee raised my right hand after my match. It was reminiscent of those matches at the Northern Tournament my junior year, when people turned their backs on the match in front of them to watch mine on the neighboring mat.

I bounded off the mat and met Coach Green behind the scorer's table, just as we did after each match. Usually, during this time, Coach Green talked a little bit about the match, while I put on my warm-ups. He wasn't talking any strategy after my final match, though.

"Trevon," he said, as he stuck out his right hand, "It's been a great year, and an absolute pleasure and honor to have you wrestle for me."

For a guy who didn't speak loudly or often, Coach Green had a way with words. I thought back to his first words to me in the hallway my junior year—how it would be an honor for me to come to open mat. It was an honor for me, too, to learn from him. A tear started to fall from my right eye, and it moved faster as I thought about the significance of this moment. This was the end. There were no more matches. There would be no more practices.

"Thanks, Coach," I said, as I shook his hand. "Thanks for everything."

We returned to our seats and watched the championship matches and the medal ceremonies that followed each one. The 103-pound final, in which Sharbaugh defeated Shilling, was the last match of the evening. Then came my chance to stand proudly among the best wrestlers in the state. I had an ear-to-ear smile from the moment I got to the arena floor, and kept it as I climbed onto the third-place stand. I received a hearty handshake from a tournament official, who presented me with a medal. I left Cole Field House that night as happy as I've ever been, my medal in hand.

12

I n December of 2005, Dan Snow watched me wrestle for the first time, unable to believe what he was hearing. He was sitting in the bleachers at Kent County High School, on the Eastern Shore of Maryland, behind two women whose sons were wrestling in the same tournament as me. The women were having a conversation about how it was totally unfair that I was wrestling opponents in the 103-pound weight class. They looked at my broad shoulders and muscular arms, and compared them to those of my lankier opponents. Mr. Snow didn't know a whole lot about wrestling. He was there to watch his stepson, Taylor Green, who wrestled for River Hill High School in Howard County. Green wound up winning the tournament's 152-pound title, and three months later finished runner-up at the state tournament for the second year in a row.

Mr. Snow listened to those women for about five minutes, and shook his head with each of their comments. He had never stepped onto a wrestling mat, and all of his knowledge of the sport came from casual conversations with his stepson. Yet he swore that those women were wrong. Finally, he had held his tongue long enough.

"Ladies," he said, "I can't believe what I'm hearing. You honestly want to sit here and say he has an advantage out there? He's got courage and guts, and he goes out there and wrestles. Would any one of you trade your kid's position with this kid?

"He can't play basketball. He can't kick a football. He found something he can do."

The ladies sat there with their jaws dropped, and their hands over their mouths, as Mr. Snow went on and on, his voice getting louder and more passionate with each sentence. The amazing thing was, he had never seen me before that day. He didn't even know my name. Apparently, though, I had an effect on him. Once he finished speaking, one of the ladies swallowed hard and said, "Mr. Snow, thank you. We hadn't thought about that. You're absolutely right. We're sorry."

Mr. Snow watched me finish second in the tournament, and then went to the gymnasium wall to look for my name and school on the bracket sheets. He went home that night and headed straight for his computer. He wanted to find out who I was, so he searched the Internet for anything with my name, and as he did so, his interest in me grew. Newspaper stories taught him a little bit about my background. He decided he wanted to do something to help me out, and so he concocted a plan.

The following week, Mr. Snow and his wife, Sharon (Taylor's mother), went to a charity dinner for Howard County General Hospital that attracted many of the county's most influential and successful businessmen. Sharon served on the event's board of directors, and Mr. Snow had met many of the event's high rollers at prior functions. He also knew many influential people on his own, from a successful business career in the Washington D.C. area for 36 years.

Mr. Snow approached J.P. Bolduc, CEO of JPB Enterprises, a venture capital and investment-banking firm, and started his sales pitch.

"J.P., I saw this kid wrestle," he said, "and let me tell you, I've never seen anyone like him."

Mr. Snow went on to describe my condition, my background—things he had learned from reading about me—and how I placed second in the tournament. Bolduc was intrigued. He had played college baseball, so he always had an interest in athletics. Given his position in the business world and his presence at this charity dinner, he was also interested in philanthropy.

"He's going to graduate from high school," Mr. Snow continued, "and then what is he going to do? He's not going to get a job as a truck driver. He's not going to lay brick. Is he going to work at a department store? He's got no family business like we have.

"The kid has three strikes against him already, and that's not fair. Number one, he was born with no legs; number two, he was born black; and number three, he was born poor. His family doesn't have the contacts, resources, or the network that we have to give him the opportunity he needs.

"He wants to do something, but he doesn't know where to go. But if he goes to college, he could be a lawyer or an accountant. Nobody in his family has gone to college, though.

"J.P., we should get a few people together and pay for this kid to go to school."

It was the most breathtaking speech anyone could have given on my behalf. Bolduc had only one answer.

"Count me in," he told Mr. Snow. "You just let me know what you need from me."

By the end of the evening, Mr. Snow had assembled a group of businessmen eager to learn more about me and what they could do to help put me through college. Mr. Snow was relieved to have the help; he had never done anything quite like this before. A few weeks later, Mr. Snow called Coach Green at Huntingtown to introduce himself, describe his plan for me, and ask to visit us at the school. He came by after a practice in mid-February. Mr. Snow told me how much my wrestling and attitude impressed him. He asked me about my grades, and I told them they were okay, but not great.

"Well, you've proven you can handle anything put in front of you," he said with a broad grin. "We will make sure you have an opportunity to go to college."

"Thank you very much, sir," I said. "But I don't understand. What have I done for you guys?"

"We were impressed enough with what you've done for yourself," he said, "and I think people ought to know about you."

I was overwhelmed, but not as much as Coach Green was; he had a hard time putting his feelings into words as he drove me home from practice that night.

"Keep your grades up," Coach Green told me, "and I'll be in contact with Mr. Snow."

I sat silently as we drove to my house. I couldn't believe it. Someone who had seen me once and had never spoken to me, introduced himself with a pledge to pay for my college education. My obligation was to take advantage of it.

"You can't finalize anything until you see it on paper," Coach Green told me, "but this is a guy who's willing to pay for you to go to college. This is an opportunity of a lifetime.

"Don't screw it up."

I got out of the car and went into my bedroom to think a little more about what this could mean for me. Not only would I be the first person in my family to go to college, but it wouldn't cost my parents a dime, either. I called my mother, who was working that evening, and told her the news. She was as stunned as I was. Those sort of charitable people didn't exist in our world. She didn't know any wealthy people, and certainly none who were this generous.

A week after the state championships in early March, Coach Green and I went to Mr. Bolduc's office in Columbia, Maryland, to meet him, three of his associates, and Mr. Snow. I was so nervous because of what was on the line. This wasn't a wrestling match or a track race; this was my future, and it depended upon how I presented myself to these generous people. As we entered the office, there were two receptionists sitting at the main desk. When we identified ourselves and said we were there to see Mr. Bolduc, one of them replied, "Oh, you're the wrestler?"

"Yes, ma'am."

"I've seen you in the newspaper. My son is a wrestler, too. We think you're terrific."

That brought a smile to my face and made me feel much more comfortable. I only grew more relaxed as we walked down a hallway toward a conference room. Mr. Bolduc pointed out huge autographed prints of President Reagan and Muhammad Ali on the walls. Before we arrived in the conference room, Mr. Bolduc took us into his office where there were several pieces of autographed sports memorabilia that decorated the walls and shelves. We casually talked about sports, which calmed my nerves even more.

We sat down at a 40-foot-long table in the conference room. Mr. Snow gave the same speech he gave Mr. Bolduc three months earlier. I had never been more flattered by someone's comments. Mr. Snow barely knew me, yet he was able to high-light the most critical parts of my identity and personality, and use them to appeal to others present that day.

Then they turned the floor over to me.

"What are your plans for college?" they asked.

My background indicated I was not destined for college. None of my older siblings ever had an interest in school once they received their high school diplomas. My mother was the same way, and my stepfather thought about trying to wrestle or play football in college, but once recruiters told him his knees were too damaged, so, too, were his plans. I certainly didn't get the aspiration to attend college from my home life.

When I was at Kettering Middle School, several of my teachers were the first ones to plant the seed in my head that college wasn't something we chose to go to; it was something we *had* to go to. They would tell us to watch television—whether it was the news or regular programs—and pay close attention to the different jobs people performed. The people with college degrees, my teachers said, were the ones with more important and better-paying jobs than those who just had high school diplomas. For a classroom of black students from a poor neighborhood, terms like "high paying" and "more powerful" almost seemed too good to be true. Many of us had never been told college was something we had to attend. But it made sense to me.

I couldn't have been more than eight or nine years old when I first saw the television show *Cops*, and I was immediately intrigued by the criminal justice system. Even though I grew up around a lot of violence, I was never attracted to that side of life. In fact, the other side appealed to me—working with the good guys to improve society. *Cops* made me consider a career as a police officer, but that was until I understood how dangerous that job could be. So I thought about other professions in our justice system. Criminal justice hit very close to home for me. Each of my three brothers had spent time in a juvenile detention hall at some point during their childhoods, and I saw a void in each of them. They weren't bad people, but they did some bad things when they were young and immature. They needed someone to help them turn their lives around and teach them to become good adult citizens.

In high school, I decided I wanted to pursue a career in criminal justice with children. I wanted to help kids who were in the same position as my brothers but had no one to turn to if they wanted to straighten themselves out. It's a lot easier to change people when they are younger and help get them on the right path. I saw the satisfaction people gained from helping me achieve all that I did; I wanted to turn the tables to feel that same fulfillment.

"That sounds good," Mr. Snow told me. "Just keep your grades up and get your applications in. Have you taken the SAT?"

Coach Green always nagged me about my grades. He never wanted me to lose focus of their importance and let either wrestling or my social life threaten my college dreams. But if there was one thing he told me to do before I graduated— above all else—it was to take the SAT. My mother had not taken the test. Before my stepfather's injuries were diagnosed, he took the SAT in order to qualify to play college ball, but that was 20 years earlier. The test had changed dramatically in the interim. To my family, the SAT was not that important. It was neither a requirement for high school graduation nor a job, and those were the two things my family cared about. It didn't matter how many times I begged them to give me the money needed to sign up for the test. They didn't understand its importance.

When it came time to sign up for the November test date during my senior year, I filled out an application online and asked my mother to give me her credit card so I could plug in the numbers. She said she would get it to me the next time she was around. She never did, and I missed the deadline. I tried to sign up for the January test, and that time, I filled out a paper application. I told my parents I needed either their credit card number or a check. They never gave me one, and I missed that date, too.

Coach Green was growing very impatient with me, and I felt helpless. I wanted to take the SAT, but paying for it was the one part I couldn't do. Sharon Seger, Kelli's mother, who worked in the school's administrative office, was also helping me prepare for college, and she pestered me about taking the SAT. She was one of the few people who knew about Mr. Snow's offer, because she answered the phone when he first called the school's main office. She was similarly overwhelmed by his gesture. "If you ever need any help, you just ask me," she always told me. "This is an opportunity that can't be missed. But you have to get all your work and tests done."

Finally, one day in February, Coach Green and Ms. Seger stopped my mother at the school and laid it on the line for her. If I didn't take the SAT, they told her, there was no way I would be able to go to a four-year college. I would have to go to a community college. There was something in their voices that scared my mother straight. She was so proud of me for my ambition to go to college and had bragged how I would be the first one in the family to do that. She knew the SAT was important, but until that moment she hadn't realized the SAT could be the decisive factor in my college plans, and, for that matter, my future.

My mother made sure I was signed up for the next exam, which was scheduled for the first week of May, less than four weeks before my graduation. It was still probably too late to apply to four-year colleges; most of them had their incoming classes filled by then. Coach Green and my guidance counselor, Angela Bell, both told me, though, that it might be better for me to spend a year at a community college to prepare for the increased workload in classes. During that year, they said, I could send in applications to four-year schools and transfer as a sophomore. Nevertheless, I was signed up to take the SAT, and I would have a test score that I could put on applications.

Unfortunately, that wasn't the last hurdle in my college application process. Even though Mr. Snow told me he and his group would cover my college tuition, he asked me to apply for financial aid and see what kind of assistance I could get from colleges. That also required my parents' help, and I was worried, because I didn't want to disappoint Mr. Snow. They needed to submit their previous tax returns to determine the amount of aid I could receive. Once again, this was another task completely foreign to my parents. They had never filled out a college application, let alone one for financial aid.

Two days passed and nothing happened, and I worried this would be another episode just like the one with the SAT. Ms. Seger told me at school that day to get my parents' tax returns, and she would come over to my house later that evening, pick me up and take me over to her place and help me fill out my financial aid forms online. Sure enough, Ms. Seger arrived at our front door, asked my mother to get her tax forms right then and give them to us. She did, and I got into Ms. Seger's car and went to her house, where we filled out my applications online and submitted them. I was so relieved to get that application filed and show Mr. Snow that he could trust me to follow his directions.

With my parents spending nearly the first six months of my senior year away from home, taking care of my stepfather's grandmother, I needed people to help me overcome my loneliness away from school. I was hanging out with Brittany Norton on a Saturday in September of my senior year. Even though she had graduated four months earlier, Brittany was enrolled at the College of Southern Maryland and lived at home with her folks. We were back at her place, and it was late.

"Is it okay if I spend the night here?" I asked her.

"We don't have any extra beds," she said. "Just a couch."

"That's fine," I replied. "Look at me. I don't need a bed."

I started to spend weekend nights with the Nortons when my parents weren't home, and they provided the family atmosphere I so desperately wanted and needed. They were kind, funny, and made me feel as if I were a part of their family at their home. I could not have asked for anything more. I was desperate for help at that time, and not only were the Nortons there to provide it, they gave more than they needed to.

Brittany also introduced me to her grandfather, Henry Huff, who was eager to meet me. Brittany had told him story after story about me since my junior year, and for good reason. Mr. Huff lost his right leg in a car accident when he was 21 years old. Yet he went on to get married, have three children, and become pastor at a nearby church.

Mr. Huff and I hit it off right away. He used crutches to walk, and we were able to share stories about overcoming the same difficulties getting around and absorbing weird looks from passersby in public. By the second time we saw one another, I began to realize that he and I shared many of the same emotions about our conditions. We talked freely about our bodies and how that drove us harder to resist pity. I began to go to his Sunday services with Brittany, and frequently he made mention of me during his sermons. It meant a lot to me for a couple hundred people to hear this man say I was an inspiration to him.

It turned out Mr. Huff was also an inspiration to me. I looked carefully at his life—his family, his career, and how happy he was—and saw that I could achieve the same things for myself in the future. It was comforting to see an example of a disabled adult enjoying a life no different from anyone else. Throughout the latter part of my childhood—essentially since the time I had quit participating in wheelchair sports—I had shunned interacting with other disabled people, because I felt that that was the way I had to prove my place alongside normal people. It was through my time with Mr. Huff that I was able to see how silly that idea was. He and I shared a very special bond. We both had overcome tremendous odds, and it gave us pride—in addition to some pleasant company—to share those experiences with one another.

I spent much of the last three months of high school thinking about my life as an adult. A week after the state championships, I was invited to an all-star exhibition meet of Maryland senior wrestlers. It was my last time in a wrestling uniform, and while some of the matches were going on, I sat in the bleachers and looked at one of my assistant coaches, Bruce Bevard, sitting to my left. With his wife next to him, Coach Bevard held their baby daughter, and that scene captured my attention. Perhaps this was something I could do. Coaching combined two of my passions—staying involved in the sport while helping kids. I could see myself with a wife and children going to meets, and treating the wrestling team like an extended family.

I also spent the month of May in an unlikely place for someone with no legs—driver's education classes. From my days competing with Air Capital, I saw that disabled people could drive. There was a device my coach at Air Capital, who was also disabled, had in his van that allowed him to use his hands to control the gas and brake pedals. I was six years old when I first saw the device, and from that moment, I knew that my disability would not prevent me from driving. As I learned how a car operates, I knew I would have no trouble learning how to use the hand controls. There are two levers that extend from the floor to the left or right of the steering wheel. One of them pushes out and away from my chest and operates the gas pedal, while the other pushes down toward the floor and manipulates the brake.

When I began high school and my friends started looking forward to getting their driver's licenses, I never hesitated to join the conversation. I was firm in my belief that I could drive, and when I explained to others how the hand controls worked, they were initially taken aback. Eventually, though, they understood how it worked, and didn't think twice about me being able to drive. I was looking forward to the summer after graduation, when I would begin taking lessons on the road with my hand controls.

Going to college, getting a job, having a family, driving a car—they were all aspects of life everyone else took for granted, and I wanted to convey that theme when I was invited to address the graduating class at the Benedictine School on Maryland's Eastern Shore. It is a small school for children and adults with developmental disabilities. A teacher at the school had read about me in a newspaper article and asked me to speak at the school's small graduation ceremony. I was honored.

I was also nervous. Except for the two or three sentences I uttered at the Wrestling Hall of Fame induction, I had never spoken to a large group of people whom I didn't know. I wanted to show that I was strong and confident, so I didn't prepare a speech, just a few notes. After the national anthem and a welcoming address, I was called to the front of the gymnasium. From my wheelchair, I looked at the dozen or so graduates and their families, and spoke for only about three minutes. That, however, was plenty of time for me to drive home two critical points.

First, I wanted to tell the story of how doctors told me when I was four or five years old that I wouldn't be able to play sports. I knew most of those kids were told many times in their lives that they couldn't try certain things. I told them to believe in themselves, and never let someone tell you that you couldn't do something. From there, I told them to look at the people with them—their families and friends. There is no way they could accomplish their dreams without those people. It was a lesson I struggled with my entire childhood, balancing my pursuit of independence with my need to have emotional support. I could tell my words hit home with that crowd. After certain sentences, I looked into the audience and saw heads nodding with approval and broad grins of acknowledgment. When I finished, everyone stood and applauded, and I felt proud, yet, once again, humbled.

But I had another graduation to think about—my own. It was a day I had looked forward to since elementary school, when people dismissed my dreams because of my condition. "You'll never graduate from high school," some of them would say because of what I couldn't do. The comments were so shallow, for they had nothing to do with my academic potential. I think people said such disparaging things because they couldn't imagine themselves with my condition. It was a motivating force earlier in my life, but by the time I got to

Huntingtown, I knew I had proven them wrong so many times over that it wasn't worth my time recalling it. I had done things they never would or could do.

Even though I had much bigger goals, there was a reason to celebrate my high school graduation. It was the culmination of my childhood and all of my incredible experiences. As much as people talk about graduation being the start of something more extraordinary, I felt it was appropriate to use the day to think back on how I got there.

The ceremony was held at the Show Place Arena, a 5,000-seat venue in Prince George's County, almost midway between Huntingtown and my old home in Capitol Heights. I thought that was appropriate, since both my identity and many achievements were born out of experiences from those two places. We lined up behind a curtain and entered the main floor in our gowns, which were baby blue, the school's official color. We emerged from the right of the stage, and found our seats among the 13 rows of chairs laid out for those graduating. I decided not to use my scooter to move around. I walked on my hands, as my gown dragged along the floor. It was my way of showing my independence at a most important moment.

There was a member of the faculty sitting on the end of each row, and it just so happened that Coach Green was sitting in my row, two seats to my left. Before we marched in, he asked me which of my family members were in attendance. I told him about my parents, my younger brother, my sister, grandmother, aunts, uncles, and cousins sitting in section 124. I was disappointed, though, that my two older brothers were unable to get time off from their jobs to attend.

"Well, I'm here for you," he said, "I'll always be here for you."

It was such a fitting way for me to celebrate my graduation. Nobody at Huntingtown was a bigger supporter or motivational force for me than Coach Green. The speeches I heard moments later during the ceremony talked a lot about the uncertainty of the future, and how nothing we have is guaranteed. Those speakers obviously did not know about my relationship with Coach Green. I listened to the speeches and tried to apply certain passages to my life—both my past and future. "With regard to the future, dream big," instructed Principal Robert Dredger. Vice Principal Dave Taylor told us, "Every one of you has the ability to do something special." These were all principles that I applied both to my days at Huntingtown and to my life beyond.

My row of classmates was called to the stage about midway through the presentation of diplomas. Each student received varying amounts of applause, usually from his or her family and friends sitting in a particular section of the arena. The announcers waited only about two seconds between calling graduates onto the stage. When my name was called, I boosted myself up the nine stairs to the stage, and I was surprised when an ovation came from the entire arena—a sound I will never forget. The school superintendent Ken Horsman handed me my diploma and then leaned over with a handshake and said, "Congratulations on a job well done." I took the diploma into my left hand and continued off stage and back to my seat.

When the ceremony ended, we proceeded behind the curtains and toward the exit behind the stage. I hopped on my scooter and rolled up a ramp to the loading dock where parents were greeting their children. I got to the top of the ramp, and there was my mother standing there in a white blouse and skirt, with tears falling down her face. She leaned over and gave me a hug that lasted for close to a minute. She sobbed as she threw her right arm around me and held me close. Even though she didn't say anything for that minute, I knew we were both thinking the same thing. She was the closest person to me in my life; she was there for me when I was young, when we were both confused and looking for direction. There was plenty we both had to overcome to find that direction and get to that moment. We had done it.

We were also both beginning to realize, though, that it was nearing the time for me to be on my own. She knew it. This was the uncertainty that I had heard in those speeches just moments before. It was May 31, and I still didn't know where I was going to college, though it appeared to be the College of Southern Maryland, a community college, for at least one year. A new candidate, however, had emerged just a couple weeks earlier, and it was an intriguing possibility.

In early May, Coach Green passed along a phone message for me that he had retrieved from the school office. It was from Jim Glatch, the wheelchair basketball coach at Edinoboro College in northwestern Pennsylvania. My name came up in a conversation between Coach Glatch and my old coach at Air Capital, and

Coach Glatch wanted to know if I was interested in playing for him. I was stunned. I thought my wheelchair basketball days were long behind me.

Coach Green couldn't have been happier for me. Not only was this an opportunity to get into a four-year college, but Edinboro was his alma mater. It was one of the freakiest things I could have imagined. He also told me how well the school accommodated its students with disabilities, who accounted for nearly 10 percent of the enrollment.

When I called Coach Glatch, I was surprised to hear him say that he remembered me from my days with Air Capital. "You were really quick," he told me. "When was the last time you played?"

"Um, five years ago," I replied.

He told me that my time off wouldn't be a problem. I had to get my application into the school's admissions department, and if I got accepted, Coach Glatch said I still had the athleticism he could coach into a successful player.

Even though I hadn't played in so long, I had learned plenty in the interim about the sport. Most importantly: that it was okay for me to play wheelchair sports and still maintain a connection to the non-disabled culture. Part of that I learned through my conversations with Henry Huff, who was proud of his condition. But I also had to experience life away from the disabled culture to grow and mature—and eventually to see that I missed it, too. When I received my acceptance letter to Edinboro at the end of June, I knew that it was okay to go back into wheelchair sports.

Even though I'll be starting all over, I am experienced with those sorts of transitions. I like to compare going to college to moving to Huntingtown, as it was such a drastic change for me. It doesn't bother me that I am going to a place where I don't know anyone and will have to make friends with people who will give me those same double-takes I've received my whole life. If anything, in fact, it might be easier for me now that I'm more mature, and the people I'll be meeting will be more mature, too. I can handle those awkward situations much better than I did when I was younger. I'll be living in a dorm, and I'll be ready for the moment my roommate walks in for the first time and sees the person he's living with has no legs.

Of course, when I first moved to Huntingtown, I was lonely and didn't know anyone. Luckily, I had my family to escape to and lean on for support. I won't have that at Edinboro. In a sense, though, I always will. My mother is so proud of me, both for my accomplishments and for my desire to continue to achieve. I took a mental image—a snapshot—of the smile I saw on her face the day of my graduation, which spoke of the pride she felt for me. I know how difficult her life has been. I want to keep making her proud, and that's the reason I am going to succeed in college and beyond. I want to see that smile every time I'm with her, just as I'll always remember the way she looked on my graduation day.

13

I was eight years old when I launched my part-time career as a philosopher.

"Mom," I asked, "Why was I born this way?"

It was a good thing my mother was sitting down. She pulled her eyes away from the television and struggled to keep the tears back. Needless to say, she wasn't prepared for that serious question to pop up out of the blue.

"Well, baby, God puts us all on this planet for a reason," she said. "Only God knows what that reason is. I think God wants you to inspire people."

"What does that mean?" I asked her.

"It means you help them to do good things."

I was confused. I went into my bedroom and looked in the mirror. This was too deep a concept for an eight-year-old to understand. I needed to learn how to inspire people. I stared at the reflection of my body and tried to find what about it would prove to be inspirational. What good things could this body do? I couldn't see anything that day. Later, I learned the most important lesson of my life from that time spent looking in the mirror: don't pass judgment on a first glance. It was a moral that resurfaced often throughout my childhood; sometimes in places I would least expect it.

Eight years later, people looked at me—a novice wrestler—with the same skepticism. They couldn't understand how a wrestler could be any good in a sport where a person's legs are so essential to success. Obviously, I proved them wrong; but at the same time, I also gave them inspiration. It shouldn't have surprised me, since I had a good track record in this department.

It began at Randall Elementary School, where my view of the world began to rapidly change. I saw things that appeared to be out of the realm of possibility for someone like me without legs. But my physical education teacher, Bob Gray, didn't see things the same way. He told me I could do the same things as people with legs, and then he showed me how. Each time I proved him right, I was further amazed and inspired by him. Through my experience with Mr. Gray, I never again looked at an activity and accepted that it was impossible without trying it first.

My attitude extended beyond physical activities. My participation in television production and dance classes at Kettering Middle School, as well as hanging out with Moo and my friends in Capitol Heights, taught me that someone with no legs can function just fine alongside people with two legs. It didn't require much sacrifice from others, just determination on my behalf. When my friends and classmates who doubted my abilities saw me participating with them, they were inspired to work harder. If they doubted me, then there was no way I should have outworked them.

It continued when I arrived at Huntingtown High School for my junior year. I appeared to be an outsider who didn't fit the profile of Calvert County. I entered high school, a place with a hierarchy firmly established and difficult to change. People with disabilities weren't supposed to become king of both Homecoming and Prom. Black kids weren't supposed to integrate into a predominantly white community and become so popular. My ability to overcome those preconceptions I hoped was inspirational to many of my classmates and friends.

Yet even as I strived to be open-minded, I could sometimes be just as closed-minded. It took me a while to realize that I was ignorant to this lesson. When my family moved out of Capitol Heights, I looked at Huntingtown, Calvert County, and the suburban life, and dismissed it all before I had even given it a fair shot. I thought I had nothing in common with anyone in the community because I looked so different than my new classmates and community members. I had to overcome my own prejudices, the same ones I fought so hard to get people to overlook when it came to me. That encouraged me to be more tolerant of people.

When I consider my childhood, I look past the obvious—the apparent curse of being born without legs—and think about the incredible strokes of luck that have been perfectly timed to give me the life I now have. Had each unfolded differently, there is a good chance I would not be where I am today.

Could there have been a more perfect teacher than Mr. Gray for me to have when I began school? He instilled in me a passion for independence and curiosity, both of which were critical for me to learn when I was a young kid. Mr. Gray would have been a great teacher at any stage in my life, but had he come along when I was 10 or 12 years old, I likely would have had different—and most likely, less ambitious—habits ingrained in me.

The people I met at Huntingtown each came along at exactly the right time. Consider how fortunate I was to have Dave Taylor as the vice principal assigned to my grade. Not only was he someone with an interest in sports, but he was once also a wrestling coach. I could have gone up to any administrator with the idea of wrestling and been discouraged. Mr. Taylor never flinched when I suggested wrestling, even if he doubted how quickly I could learn the sport. He introduced me to Coach Terry Green, and how lucky was I to have him in my corner? Some coaches could have seen the burden of coaching someone like me—not just with my disability, but coupled with my total inexperience—and said "forget about it." His patience, generosity, and dedication to teaching were a package of traits that come along in the same person once in a lifetime.

It was perfect that the first two classmates I met at Huntingtown were Jessie Moulton and Alyssa Finlayson. My conversation with them steered me down a social path at the school that I probably would not have considered without their nudge. Instead of flocking toward Huntingtown's few black students and being alienated from the rest, I saw that I could find friends among the people with whom I appeared to have the least in common.

Huntingtown itself was the perfect school for me. It's tough enough for a teenager to change high schools because there is an already established social structure at the new school that can prove difficult to break into. But there was no such structure at Huntingtown, because it was a new school. The entire student body had to find its place. Everyone started at the same level in seeking his or her niche at the school. My place happened to be the wrestling mat, a forum I used to propel myself to acceptance and the kind of opportunities I never could have imagined. I only spent two years with the sport, yet it affected me more than anything else in my previous 16 years, and it will be very difficult to leave behind.

After years of being told I was different, all I wanted was to be seen as normal. Wrestling proved to be the perfect equalizer. I was alone on the mat with my opponent. There was no outside variable that I could use as a crutch. If I were to succeed, I would have to do it on the same terms as a normal person who wrestled. I can't think of another sport that could have satisfied my desire to be seen as normal any better.

Throughout the postseason of my senior year, people told me what a bright future I had in wrestling because of how quickly I learned the sport. They told me that some wrestlers who spend a decade in the sport never place as high as I did at the state tournament. I believe them, and I do wonder how good I could have become with some more training and experience. I also wonder if it will be a challenge to be treated normally without wrestling in my life.

People ask me if I am done with wrestling, and I tell them that collegiate wrestling opportunities are continuing to disappear, as schools have chosen to cut back on wrestling programs in order to comply with Title IX, the law mandating gender equity in all federally funded institutions. Edinboro happens to have a wrestling program, but my plan is to play wheelchair basketball. If I do have an itch to wrestle, though, I know at least one Edinboro wrestling alumnus who will lobby his alma mater to give me a shot.

But I am eager to see what I can gain from wheelchair basketball as an adult, just as I'm excited to pursue a career in criminal justice. Wrestling was a marvelous vehicle to help me establish myself in a new community. All the success was just a bonus, as was the effect my wrestling had on others.

As much as I will miss the emotional satisfaction I gained from wrestling, I'm also going to miss the attention. For so much of my childhood, people looked at me with curiosity because I wasn't normal and didn't fit in with the way every-one else looked. Wrestling focused people's eyes right on me because of my accomplishments, and I loved holding their interest. After my senior wrestling season, people who I didn't know would stop me in the street at least once a week and con-gratulate me on placing third in the state tournament. It was a thrilling feeling. I was famous and I loved that. In my adult life, though, I don't know what other activities could garner me the celebrity I gained from wrestling.

I suppose I might have to I just live life as a normal person. That wouldn't be too bad, either.